JOURNAL OF
M·O·R·A·L
THEOLOGY

VOLUME 8, NUMBER 1
JANUARY 2019

CATHOLIC HEALTH MINISTRY

Edited by
Rachelle Barina
Nathaniel Hibner
Tobias Winright

JOURNAL · OF
M · O · R · A · L
THEOLOGY

Journal of Moral Theology is published semiannually, with regular issues in January and June. Our mission is to publish scholarly articles in the field of Catholic moral theology, as well as theological treatments of related topics in philosophy, economics, political philosophy, and psychology.

Articles published in the *Journal of Moral Theology* undergo at least two double blind peer reviews. Authors are asked to submit articles electronically to jmt@msmary.edu. Submissions should be prepared for blind review. Microsoft Word format preferred. The editors assume that submissions are not being simultaneously considered for publication in another venue.

Journal of Moral Theology is available full text in the *ATLA Religion Database with ATLASerials®* (RDB®), a product of the American Theological Library Association.
Email: atla@atla.com, www: http://www.atla.com.

ISSN 2166-2851 (print)
ISSN 2166-2118 (online)

Journal of Moral Theology is published by Mount St. Mary's University, 16300 Old Emmitsburg Road, Emmitsburg, MD 21727.

Copyright© 2019 individual authors and Mount St. Mary's University. All rights reserved.

Except for brief quotations in critical publications or reviews, no part of this book may be reproduced in any manner without prior written permission from the publisher. Write: Permissions. Wipf and Stock Publishers, 199 W. 8th Ave., Suite 3, Eugene, OR 97401.

Pickwick Publications, An Imprint of Wipf and Stock Publishers, 199 W. 8th Ave., Suite 3, Eugene, OR 97401. www.wipfandstock.com. ISBN 13: 978-1-5326-7922-3

JOURNAL OF
M·O·R·A·L
THEOLOGY

EDITOR EMERITUS AND UNIVERSITY LIAISON
David M. McCarthy, *Mount St. Mary's University*

EDITOR
Jason King, *Saint Vincent College*

SENIOR EDITOR
William J. Collinge, *Mount St. Mary's University*

ASSOCIATE EDITOR
M. Therese Lysaught, *Loyola University Chicago*

MANAGING EDITOR
Kathy Criasia, *Mount St. Mary's University*

BOOK REVIEW EDITORS
Kent Lasnoski, *Quincy University*
Christopher McMahon, *Saint Vincent College*

EDITORIAL BOARD
Jana M. Bennett, *University of Dayton*
Mara Brecht, *St. Norbert College*
Jim Caccamo, *St. Joseph's University*
Meghan Clark, *St. John's University*
David Cloutier, *The Catholic University of America*
Christopher Denny, *St. John's University*
Matthew Gaudet, *Santa Clara University*
Mari Rapela Heidt, *Waukesha, Wisconsin*
Kelly Johnson, *University of Dayton*
Andrew Kim, *Marquette University*
Warren Kinghorn, *Duke University*
John Love, *Mount St. Mary's Seminary*
Ramon Luzarraga, *Benedictine University, Mesa*
William C. Mattison III, *University of Notre Dame*
Christopher McMahon, *Saint Vincent College*
Mary M. Doyle Roche, *College of the Holy Cross*
Joel Shuman, *Kings College*
Matthew Shadle, *Marymount University*
Christopher P. Vogt, *St. John's University*
Brian Volck, *University of Cincinnati College of Medicine*
Paul Wadell, *St. Norbert College*
Greg Zuschlag, *Oblate School of Theology*

JOURNAL OF MORAL THEOLOGY
VOLUME 8, NUMBER 1
JANUARY 2019

CONTENTS

A Note from the Editors
Rachelle Barina, Nathaniel Hibner, Tobias Winright 1

Repair Work: Rethinking the Separation of Academic Moral Theologians and Catholic Health Care Ethicists
Paul J. Wojda 4

Catholic Bioethicists and Moral Theologians Drifting Apart?: A Sequela of Specialization and Professionalization
Becket Gremmels 22

Equally Strange Fruit: Catholic Health Care and the Appropriation of Residential Segregation
Cory D. Mitchell and M. Therese Lysaught 36

Does Hospital and Health System Consolidation Serve The Common Good?
Michael Panicola 63

Accompaniment with the Sick: An Authentic Christian Vocation that Rejects the Fallacy of Prosperity Theology
Ramon Luzarraga 76

Grace at the End of Life: Rethinking Ordinary and Extraordinary Means in a Global Context
Conor Kelly 89

A Voice in the Wilderness: Reimagining the Role of Catholic Health Care Mission Leader
Michael McCarthy 114

Theologians in Catholic Healthcare Ministries: Breaking Beyond the Bond with Ethics
Darren M. Henson 130

Contributors 145

A Note from the Editors

Rachelle Barina, Nathaniel Hibner, and Tobias Winright

THIS SPECIAL ISSUE of the *Journal of Moral Theology* brings moral theologians and health care ethicists together to explore current topics in Catholic health care ethics. Catholic health care organizations have grown into ministries of unprecedented size, complexity, and power, and the ethicists and mission leaders that they employ are enmeshed in clinical and organizational questions that have theological importance. Throughout the development of organized U.S. health care, moral theologians have been fruitfully engaged in scholarship and dialogue about medico-moral matters, and moral theologians have moved between the academy and mission and ethics roles in health ministry. In bringing scholars and ethicists together, this issue explores the evolution of their relationship and opportunities to further partner in serving the Catholic moral tradition and the church's health ministry. It also highlights a number of papers that are of topical relevance to the changing health care landscape today.

As editors, we hoped that this issue would include papers from both moral theologians and health care ethicists, and we did achieve some balance. (Although we wish we had more balance with regard to the gender of authors, as well as experience and seniority.) The issue opens with two papers that explore the roles of each group and the opportunities to partner together, one written by moral theologian Paul Wojda and the second by ethicist Becket Gremmels. The issue continues with four papers that explore topics of moral significance in Catholic health ministry: Cory Mitchell and Therese Lysaught on residential segregation, Michael Panicola on the impact of mergers and acquisitions, Ramon Luzarraga on prosperity theology, and Conor Kelley on global solidarity in end of life decision-making. Finally, the issue concludes with papers from Michael McCarthy and Darren Henson, both of whom assess the current professional landscape and point towards the vast opportunities for theologians to contribute to health ministries. On the whole, we hope that this issue will increase our mutual interest in and understanding of one another.

We also want to note some of the shortfalls we experienced in the process of collecting these essays. First, we were not overwhelmed by a large number of submissions or vast amount of interest in writing for this issue. Perhaps this substantiates the need for dialogue and increased collaboration that prompted us to organize the issue in the first place. We hope that this issue might encourage more interest in health ministry during the vocational exploration of theologians as well as more literature that engages Catholic medico-moral matters and moral questions about health care systems and organizations.

Second, some topics we hoped to include were not covered. For example, we hoped to include an in depth examination of the importance and necessary scope of theological training for mission/ethics leaders in health ministry. We also hoped for interest in the topic of academic freedom and the roles of academic theologians and Catholic health care leaders in negotiating controversial moral matters. There has long been discussion about the role of theologians in controversial moral matters, but there is no scholarship on the experiences of ethicists and mission leaders, whose writing is sometimes being constrained or censored. There is need for further discussion about how academic theologians and ethicists might collaborate on ensuring there is a healthy level of theological discourse and scholarship on the controversial moral matters that ethicists are often experiencing in real time, long before broader discussion in the public or church.

As a final note, we want to be so bold as to acknowledge that in our personal experiences as well as in discussing this special issue with both theologians and mission/ethics leaders, we have been surprised by the strong sentiments held by some members in each group about the other. We sense a suspicion from some theologians about whether the academic and practical work of Catholic health care ethics is in fact a rigorous application of the theological tradition. We also have encountered more than a few ethicists who criticize moral theologians for not being more engaged in Catholic health ministry or more attuned to the practical realities of clinical care, organizational affairs, and health policy. Neither point was made explicitly in any of the articles, but these sentiments loom in subtle, unspoken, yet influential ways in perceptions of theologians and health care mission/ethics leaders. These sentiments illustrate the need for ongoing dialogue so that each group can understand and support the work of the other. The two roles are different ways of living the vocation of the theologian, and both are important in the life of a healthy and vibrant church that has large educational and healing ministries.

As theologians and mission/ethics leaders, we all have our existing interests and commitments, and we all tend to remain focused in those areas where we are comfortable and knowledgeable. Catholic universities, starting with theologians, and Catholic health ministry, starting with mission/ethics leaders, have an opportunity to improve and maximize our collaboration. The opportunities are vast, stemming from university programs preparing people for health professions, the many

PhD trained theologians who struggle to find adequate employment, and the sincere challenges of health care today that would benefit from the attention of people committed to social justice and the common good. Catholic universities and health ministries can support and feed one another, ensuring a vibrancy in our intellectual traditions as well as our service traditions. As theologians and mission/ethics leaders, let's lead the way with this collaboration in shared service of our Catholic moral and social vision.

We also would like to thank graduate student Addison Tenorio for her assistance with this project. ∎

… Journal of Moral Theology, Vol. 8, No. 1 (2019): 4-21

Repair Work:
Rethinking the Separation of Academic Moral Theologians and Catholic Health Care Ethicists

Paul J. Wojda

DESPITE CONSIDERABLE OVERLAP in requisite knowledge, skills, and even job responsibilities, moral theologians working in Catholic colleges and universities and health care ethicists working in Catholic health care organizations have tended to operate in parallel worlds.[1] It is a division of labor in many ways both old and new, but one whose wisdom has recently been called into question. Ought there to be a closer relationship between academic moral theologians and Catholic health care ethicists? If so, what form might that relationship take? The following essay takes up both questions. Its concluding section roughly outlines one possible form such closer collaboration might take, using as a model the ACE ("Alliance for Catholic Education") program established in the early 1990s at the University of Notre Dame. The intervening sections constitute the necessary historical and theological prolegomena to that proposal.

Any proposal for closer collaboration between the worlds of academic moral theology and Catholic health care ethics must answer three distinct but related questions. First, in the current division of labor between academic moral theology and Catholic health care ethics, what is essential and what is accidental? Second, in what respects would closer collaboration be beneficial to both sides of this relationship? Put somewhat differently, what does academic moral theology have to teach Catholic health care ethics, and conversely, what does Catholic health care ethics have to teach academic moral theology? Third, can adequate *theological grounds* for such a collaboration be articulated, and if so, what might they look like?

---

[1] In what follows I use the term "academic moral theologian" to refer to persons working primarily in departments of theology within Catholic universities. I use the term "health care ethicist" to refer to those working in Catholic health care organizations. I use the term "Catholic health care organization" to refer to any structure, e.g., hospital, clinic, long-term care facility, insurer, management office, etc., that is part of a Catholic health care system.

The importance of articulating the possible theological grounds for a closer relationship between academic moral theology and Catholic health care ethics should not be gainsaid. To do so would risk letting the issue of collaboration be framed in primarily pragmatic terms. For example, it would appear that the need for Catholic health care ethicists will soon be dire. According to a recent study by the Catholic Health Association, more than two thirds of currently active Catholic health care ethicists will be retiring in the next ten to fifteen years.[2] Most of these soon-to-be-retired ethicists, as Carl Middleton writes, "have been theologians with doctorates in philosophy or sacred theology. Most...but not all, are clergy, former clergy, members of religious communities, or have been members of religious communities or seminary-trained."[3] Since these institutional contexts no longer play the role in theological formation they once did, it is natural to turn to academic moral theologians as a "potential resource," as Middleton puts it.[4]

For its part, academic moral theology, and academic theology generally, might find closer connection with Catholic health care ethics (and Catholic health care organizations generally) to their advantage, as theology departments in many Catholic colleges and universities continue to shrink due to the current reorientation of these institutions away from their historically liberal arts focus and towards professional (i.e., career) preparation.[5] In fact, given current trends, it is not unreasonable to think that, over the next two decades, for newly degreed masters and doctors of moral theology, there will be more job opportunities in Catholic health care than in Catholic higher education. If one widens the lens to include jobs in Mission Integration, and not simply positions in ethics, then this is likely already the case.

Such pragmatic considerations are not entirely irrelevant, of course, but focusing on them risks obscuring the more fundamental normative questions informing the desire to cultivate closer relationships between academic moral theology and health care ethics, questions both vocational and institutional. The vocational question concerns the identity of both academic moral theology and health care ethics, what in each case it means and requires to be a Catholic moral theologian or health care ethicist. The institutional question, closely

---

[2] Carl Middleton, "Preparing the Next Corps of Ethicists," *Health Progress* 97, no. 6 (2016): 62.
[3] Middleton, "Preparing the Next Corps of Ethicists," 65.
[4] Middleton, "Preparing the Next Corps of Ethicists," 66. Middleton recognizes the limitations of a strictly academic background, namely the lack of both clinical experience and (often) spiritual formation.
[5] See the recent *Commonweal* exchange between Massimo Faggioli and Michael Hollerich, "Do Catholic Theology Departments have a Future?" *Commonweal*, May 18, 2018, www.commonwealmagazine.org/do-catholic-theology-departments-have-future.

6   Paul J. Wojda

connected to the vocational, concerns the identity of the organizations in which these vocations are practiced. What is or ought a Catholic university to be? What is or ought a Catholic health system to be? These questions are ultimately theological questions. Neither is new, of course, and possible answers to both abound. What *does* seem to be new, though, is that academic moral theologians and Catholic health care ethicists are beginning to think afresh about them and are doing so together.

SEPARATED AT BIRTH?
   The current division of labor between academic moral theology and Catholic health care ethics would appear to be justified, in the first place, by essential differences in the nature of the institutions within which each operates and finds its distinctive role, on the one hand the Catholic university, and on the other, the Catholic health care organization. The Catholic university, as *Ex Corde Ecclesia* puts it, serves "the *cause of truth*" (no. 4). In so doing, the Catholic university also serves simultaneously the good of both the human person and the Church, for it is among the fundamental tasks of the Church to proclaim the fullness of the truth about the human person as that is known in the light of faith. Within the *universitas magistrorum et scholarium*, inspired by the love of learning and dedicated to the cause of truth, moral theologians have the specific responsibility of reflecting, from the unique and irreducible "perspective and orientation" of Christian faith, on the specifically ethical dimensions of scholarly research and the implications of its discoveries for human flourishing. This reflection is particularly needed, *Ex Corde* adds, where science and technology are concerned. For

> [i]t is essential that we be convinced of the priority of the ethical over the technical, of the primacy of the person over things, of the superiority of the spirit over matter. The cause of the human person will only be served if knowledge is joined to conscience. Men and women of science will truly aid humanity only if they preserve the sense of the transcendence of the human person over the world and of God over the human person (*Ex Corde Ecclesiae*, no. 18).

Such a task requires of the moral theologian specialized knowledge and skills: knowledge of and ability to distinguish among and interpret the authoritative texts of the tradition, including authoritative interpretations of those texts; a sensitivity to and facility with the varying forms of argument on display in those texts and their interpretations; and familiarity with the subject matters, methods, and arguments of other arts and sciences dedicated to the pursuit of knowledge and enhancement of human life, including medicine.[6]

In contrast to Catholic universities, Catholic health care organizations have as their fundamental mission the promotion of *health,* specifically the physical, mental, and spiritual health of the individuals who entrust themselves to the care of these organizations and the health of the communities in which these organizations are located.[7] Of course, because health is among those goods integral to the flourishing of both persons and communities, the full measure of which the Church seeks to promote, the Catholic health care organization will also, like the Catholic university, serve the good of both persons and the Church. Health care ethicists working within these organizations today contribute to this service in multiple ways, among other things, by advising on ethical issues that arise on both the clinical and broader operational levels; by overseeing processes designed to protect subjects of medical research; and by coordinating and conducting educational and other formation activities for the wide variety of constituencies within these organizations (e.g., medical and nursing professionals; executive leadership; boards of trustees). The knowledge, skills, and abilities necessary for carrying out these tasks are correspondingly varied, but, at their core, they include such things as knowledge of the Catholic moral tradition and, especially, the tradition of Catholic social teaching; knowledge of bioethical law and policy, and clinical and organizational ethics; an understanding of the *Ethical and Religious Directives for Catholic Health Care Services;* familiarity with the mission and charism of the organization's founding communities; and the ability to apply Catholic moral teaching to medical, social, and management issues.[8]

Based only on these lists of their respective responsibilities, which appear to have quite a bit in common, one might reasonably conclude that the line separating the work of academic moral theologians and Catholic health care ethicists is vanishingly thin, regardless of the fact that their specific institutions are ordered to distinct goods. However, it is just this distinction of institutional goods that keeps us from that

---

[6] On this list of competencies, see Michael J. Buckley, *The Catholic University as Promise and Project* (Washington, DC: Georgetown University Press, 1998), 172-182.

[7] See, for example, United States Conference of Catholic Bishops, "Part One: The Social Responsibility of Catholic Health Care Services," in *The Ethical and Religious Directives for Catholic Health Care Services,* www.usccb.org/about/doctrine/ethical-and-religious-directives/upload/ethical-religious-directives-catholic-health-service-sixth-edition-2016-06.pdf.

[8] This list is adapted from *Striving for Excellence in Ethics: A Resource for the Catholic Health Ministry, Second Edition* (St. Louis: Catholic Health Association, 2014), Appendix A.

conclusion, for that distinction also allows a second essential difference between the two vocations to come forward, one based on their respective degrees of participation in the realization of each good. Academic moral theologians, precisely as teachers and scholars (*magistri et scholares*), might be said to participate more directly, even immediately, in the good of truth constitutive of a university, so much so that a university without teachers and scholars, including moral theologians in Catholic universities, would be a contradiction in terms. Health care ethicists, on the other hand, do not seem to participate as immediately in the good of health. Health care ethicists typically have not been trained, *qua ethicists,* in the science and art of clinical judgment—the "healing relationship"—constitutive of the medical profession.[9] They are not, so to speak, *healers*. In contrast to the relationship between Catholic universities and moral theologians, it is possible to imagine a Catholic health care organization without health care ethicists, regardless of how important the position of health care ethicist has become for the operation of Catholic health care services today. The point here is not that academic moral theologians are more "essential" than health care ethicists but rather that functional differences within their respective institutions—based on the degree of participation in the good served by these institutions—constitute the clearest grounds for arguing that the distinction between the two professions is *essential* and not simply accidental.[10]

Still other distinctions might be said to justify the sharp division of labor between moral theologians and health care ethicists. Whereas academic moral theologians focus principally, though of course not exclusively, on the fundamental, "metaethical" aspects of research in the life-sciences and medicine or are concerned mainly with issues in the "cultural" and "foundational" spheres of bioethics, health care ethicists focus on "applied" issues in medicine, and accordingly restrict themselves to the "clinical" or the "law and policy" spheres of bioethics.[11]

If none of these distinctions is entirely convincing then it is likely because the circumstances that have given rise to the current division

---

[9] See Edmund Pellegrino, "The Healing Relationship: The Architectonics of Clinical Medicine," in *The Clinical Encounter,* ed. Earl E. Shelp (Dordrecht, Holland: D Reidel, 1983), 153-172.

[10] Another way of putting this difference is to note that the profession of health care ethicist is *already* a collaborative profession (as the profession of academic moral theologian is not), and not only with medical and nursing professions, but also with the full range of contemporary health care professions, by some accounts well over two hundred in number.

[11] See Daniel Callahan, "Bioethics" in *The Encyclopedia of Bioethics, Revised Edition,* ed. Warren Reich (New York: Simon & Schuster Macmillan, 1995). Also see John H. Evans, *The History and Future of Bioethics: A Sociological View* (New York: Oxford University Press, 2012), 3-74.

of labor between academic moral theology and health care ethics, which these distinctions might justify in theory, seem only loosely connected to them in practice. Rather, the division seems to have far more to do with the contingent historical events that have shaped, and which continue to shape, institutions of both Catholic higher education and Catholic health care in the United States. Attending to that history has the additional benefit of helping us understand why further collaboration might be beneficial to both, and what form that collaboration might take.

A detailed treatment of that history is beyond the scope of this essay. However, even a cursory glance would reveal that the current division of labor between academic moral theology and health care ethics is neither deeply rooted nor longstanding. In fact, a case could be made that the academic moral theologian and the health care ethicist are the twin children of a single parent: the seminary professor of moral theology who until the 1960s was the individual primarily entrusted with the responsibilities now exercised by his two offspring in the academic and health care settings. By far the most prominent individual to occupy this position was Gerald A. Kelly, S.J. (1902-64), sometimes referred to as the "father of American Catholic medical ethics."[12] Kelly received his doctorate from the Gregorian University in 1937 and taught moral theology to Jesuit scholastics at St. Mary's College (Kansas) from 1948 until his untimely death just as the Second Vatican Council was ending. During an immensely productive ten-year period (1948-1958) he performed many other duties, such as editing *Review for Religious*, and writing the regular "Notes on Moral Theology" section of the journal *Theological Studies*. However, his most notable achievement, as far as health care ethics is concerned, was as chief medical ethics advisor to the Catholic Hospital Association. It was in this capacity that Kelly wrote the first editions of what would later become the *Ethical and Religious Directives for Catholic Health Care Services*.[13]

Kelly's immediate successor, both as the editor of the "Notes on Moral Theology" for *Theological Studies* and as ethics advisor to the (renamed) Catholic Health Association, was Richard A. McCormick, S.J. (1922-2000). He was a truly transitional figure, perhaps the last of his kind, because he was both an academic moral theologian and a health care ethicist *par excellence*. McCormick, like Kelly, also received his doctorate at the Gregorian (1957), but he returned to teach

---

[12] See Kate Jackson, "Lessons from Gerald Kelly, S.J., the Father of American Catholic Medical Ethics," *Health Care Ethics USA* 23, no. 2 (2015): 7-16. See also, Paul J. Wojda, "Gerald Kelly, S.J., and the Future of Catholic Bioethics," *Theology Matters* 2, no. 2 (2016): www.stthomas.edu/theology/publications/newsletter/vol2no2/geraldkelly/.
[13] Gerald A. Kelly, S.J., *Medico-Moral Problems* (St. Louis: The Catholic Health Association, 1958).

in the United States under far different circumstances. To begin with, he spent the majority of his career in an academic, not a seminary, setting.[14] Secondly, by the early 1960s, the renewal of Catholic moral theology, which had begun in Europe more than three decades earlier, was well underway and, in fact, had been given a major boost by the Second Vatican Council's explicit call for that renewal (*Optatam Totius*, no. 16).[15] McCormick would become one of its chief American contributors.

These years mark the true origins of academic moral theology in the United States, as McCormick and many others sought to make good on the Council's challenge to identify an alternative to the dominant neo-scholasticism (and "ecclesiastical positivism") of manualists like Kelly, an alternative more deeply immersed in Scripture and accordingly more responsive to a Church newly alive to its identity as a pilgrim people within history.[16] Fundamental questions naturally rose to the top of the moral theological agenda, with the question of methodological pluralism above all and McCormick's own methodological alternative, "proportionalism," at the center of debate for the next three decades.[17]

At the same time, McCormick was also busy contributing to, or rather *creating*, Catholic health care ethics, which, like its sibling academic moral theology, also emerged in these decades (1970s-80s) as a response to a set of challenges. McCormick was well placed to respond to these challenges, especially after 1974, when he was named the Rose F. Kennedy Professor of Christian Ethics at the Kennedy Institute of Ethics at Georgetown University, a position he occupied until 1986. At Georgetown and the Kennedy Institute, McCormick was at the intersection of Catholic medical ethics, Georgetown being one of five Catholic universities with an affiliated medical school, and the emerging field of "bioethics," the Kennedy Institute, founded in 1971, one of the earliest of the new field's custodial "think-tanks." In fact, given McCormick's influence, it would not be inaccurate to see the origins of "Catholic health care ethics"— a term which only came into

---

[14] McCormick's first institutional assignment was at the Jesuit seminary (no longer in existence) at West Baden College, Indiana, then at Bellarmine School of Theology at Loyola University Chicago.

[15] Note that, even as late as the Council, moral theology was still considered primarily to be under clerical jurisdiction. For an overview of this history, see James F. Keenan, *A History of Catholic Moral Theology in the Twentieth Century: From Confessing Sins to Liberating Consciences* (New York: Continuum, 2010).

[16] On "ecclesiastical positivism," see David Kelly, *The Emergence of Roman Catholic Medical Ethics in North America* (New York: Mellen Press, 1979). On the problematic theology of neo-scholastic manuals, see Vincent McNamara, *Faith and Ethics: Recent Roman Catholicism* (Washington, DC: Georgetown University Press, 1985), 1-10.

[17] See Richard McCormick, *The Critical Calling: Reflections on Moral Dilemmas Since Vatican II* (Washington, DC: Georgetown University Press, 1988), 147-162.

Repair Work 11

wide usage at the end of the 1970s—as the consequence of his efforts to expand the scope of traditional Catholic "medical ethics" in light of the many new issues then being addressed under the heading of "bioethics," a term also first coined early in that decade.[18]

Accordingly, McCormick's contributions to Catholic health care ethics during this period covered a wide spectrum of ethical issues, virtually all of them provoked in some fashion by the secularizing forces then transforming Catholic health care in the United States, in many instances raising questions about whether a distinctive Catholic health care ministry could be sustained. Among the more important of these secularizing forces were the increasing involvement of the federal government in regulating health care in the United States, as well as the growing cultural acceptance of expanding individual liberties around a range of practices at the beginning and end of life (e.g., contraception, abortion, assisted reproductive technologies, physician-assisted suicide, euthanasia).

Deregulation of the health care marketplace in the 1980s brought still further challenges, as Catholic health care facilities joined the wave of mergers and consolidations overtaking the American health care landscape in general.[19] In order to survive, many Catholic hospitals began partnering with secular providers, very few of whom shared a commitment to traditional Catholic medical ethics in its entirety (especially on reproductive issues). On top of all this, increasing numbers of Catholic lay people (and those who professed other faiths, or no faith at all) were moving into positions of leadership within Catholic health care. Many of these positions had once been occupied by religious women, whose orders had built and maintained Catholic hospitals for much of the preceding century and a half, but who, in the wake of the changes initiated both within women's religious orders during the 1950s and by the Second Vatican Council, were not effectively replacing themselves.[20] Navigating all of these challenges would eventually become a full-time job, beyond even the considerable talents of McCormick (or most academic moral theologians). Such a task would require the development of a more specialized knowledge and set of skills. In short, it would require the services of the Catholic health care ethicist.

To summarize, then, by the end of McCormick's long career—and, coincidentally the end of the twentieth century—the now familiar division of labor between academic moral theology and Catholic health

---

[18] "Health care ethics," like "bioethics," was not a term in wide circulation until the end of the 1970s.
[19] See Arnold S. Relman, "The New Medical-Industrial Complex," *New England Journal of Medicine* 303, no. 17 (1980): 963-970.
[20] See Barbra Mann Wall, *American Catholic Hospitals: A Century of Changing Markets and Missions* (New Brunswick: Rutgers University Press, 2011), 1-22.

care ethics had fully emerged. It was not primarily a result of any essential differences between the two vocations but rather a consequence of the intra- and extra-ecclesial transformations, both cultural and institutional, in the decades immediately before and after the Second Vatican Council. These transformations were raising acute questions for both Catholic universities *and* Catholic health care organizations, primarily about identity and mission. Academic moral theologians and Catholic health care ethicists each found themselves engaging these questions, though in starkly different ways and largely independently of each other.

For academic moral theologians the fundamental, "metaethical" questions had become acute. Pursuit of these questions, however, tended to draw moral theologians—and theology departments generally—away from concerns regarding the identity and mission of Catholic universities and colleges.[21] For Catholic health care ethicists, in contrast, the challenges were less fundamental than practical. The reforms of Vatican II, and the development of Catholic social thought, provided a direction and framework for moving forward. The question for Catholic health care organizations was how to implement that vision and framework within structures whose oversight was quickly passing from religious sisters into the hands of public, juridic persons and lay boards of trustees. "Mission formation" became the byword. Given these different trajectories, it was not clear that academic moral theologians and Catholic health care ethicists had strong reasons for dialogue with each other.

As something of a coda to this history, it is useful to consider how the division between academic moral theologians and Catholic health care ethicists is illustrated in one of McCormick's final essays on the topic of Catholic health care, an essay entitled "The Catholic Hospital Today: Mission Impossible?" which McCormick originally delivered as a lecture at the Kennedy Institute in 1995.[22] It is a bleak assessment of the (then) current state of Catholic health care in the United States, as McCormick saw it. His basic claim is that the once robust culture of Catholic health care, sustained for over 150 years by a variety of institutions and individuals, the sisters above all, was in disarray. In fact, it was in danger of disappearing altogether, victim to a variety of powerful forces at work in late twentieth century American culture generally and in American medicine and health care in particular.[23]

---

[21] James F. Keenan has recently drawn attention back to these issues, *University Ethics: How Colleges Can Build and Benefit from a Culture of Ethics* (New York: Rowman & Littlefield Publishers, 2015).
[22] Richard McCormick, "The Catholic Hospital Today: Mission Impossible?" *Origins* 24, No. 39 (1995): 648-653.
[23] McCormick, "The Catholic Hospital Today," 653, summarizes these forces as follows: "1. A depersonalized atmosphere. 2. Where medicine is increasingly viewed and lived as a business. 3. At a time of powerful market and competitive pressures

Noble proclamations of Catholic identity at the institutional level (e.g., "beautiful mission statements") could not conceal the perplexity and doubt that McCormick was hearing expressed at the rank-and-file level, with many Catholics "wondering...whether they ought to be in health care, asking about their identity, how they differ from non-Catholic institutions."[24] To these questions McCormick's essay offers no answers. (The bulk of the essay is largely devoted to a more detailed description of each of the eight culture- and morale-sapping forces he identifies.) If anything, McCormick's own concluding sentences simply echo the perplexity and doubt of the rank-and-file: "How do we save the souls of these institutions .... That is my question too." It is an odd question for McCormick, of all people, to ask, given the fact that health care ethicists and mission leaders had already been working for some time to further the legacy of the sisters and were doing far more than simply writing high-minded mission statements. Is it possible that McCormick, academic moral theologian, had lost touch with their work? Some did not hesitate to say so, as Kevin O'Rourke reported in a gentle riposte to McCormick in the pages of *Health Progress*.[25]

A MUTUALLY BENEFICIAL COLLABORATION?
The burden of the previous section has been to suggest that the division of labor between academic moral theologians and Catholic health care ethicists is not founded on any insuperable differences between the two vocations but rather on a series of contingent historical events. If this is the case then it may be possible to imagine forms of collaboration between the two that, while still respecting their unique roles and responsibilities, might help each to engage more fruitfully with the ongoing challenges—ecclesial and cultural—that marked their emergence in the first place. As just noted, in both cases those challenges are primarily *institutional* in nature. That is, the fundamental question facing both academic moral theologians and Catholic health care ethicists is how they might best help their respective institutions—the university and the health care organization—contribute to the integral good of the communities, in particular the civic communities, that they serve.

Since a working awareness of this question has, on the whole, tended to be far more pronounced among Catholic health care ethicists than academic moral theologians, it is not impertinent to propose that

---

that exit patients quicker and sicker. 4. In a culture that tries to transcend mortality, invests big time in sick care and medicalizes more basic human problems. 5. At a time of the hospital's diminishing importance and religious influence."
[24] McCormick, "The Catholic Hospital Today," 648.
[25] Kevin O'Rourke, "Making Mission Possible: A Response to Rev. Richard A. McCormick's Article on the Preservation of Catholic Hospitals," *Health Progress* 76, no. 6 (1995): 46.

one of the primary benefits of closer collaboration for academic moral theologians is to be reminded of what *Ex Corde Ecclesiae* already affirms about the necessarily *social* dimensions of a Catholic university's mission.

> Every Catholic University feels responsible to contribute concretely to the progress of the society within which it works: for example it will be capable of searching for ways to make university education accessible to all those who are able to benefit from it, especially the poor or members of minority groups who customarily have been deprived of it. (no. 37)

It will be objected that academic moral theologians, in addition to, or often as part of their teaching, research, and service activities, *already* engage in a wide variety of such social service, often conjointly with civic organizations, non-profits, churches, and other religious associations. While this is doubtlessly true, it is also true that few of these other organizations are as large, as old, or as committed to a distinctively Catholic vision of their mission as are Catholic health care organizations.

It is also true that few institutions—religious or otherwise—are as connected to the actual conditions of their communities as are health care organizations, non-profit health care organizations in particular. This connection was significantly augmented, one might even say "incentivized," by the passage of the Affordable Care Act (2010), which mandated that, in order to maintain their tax-exempt status, all such hospitals must conduct triennial "Community Health Needs Assessments" (CHNA), and on that basis establish implementation plans (CHIP) to address those needs.[26] There is no single model for undertaking the CHNA/CHIP process, and thus a diversity of approaches exists, even among Catholic health care organizations. However, when done well, the entire process is undertaken as part of the health care organization's overall strategic plan and is accordingly informed by its distinctive mission, vision, and values, among which are the principles of Catholic social teaching.[27]

---

[26] All of these CHNAs and CHIPs are available online, typically linked on the home page of a hospital's website.

[27] CHRISTUS St. Vincent's Regional Medical Center is a particularly good example of a CHNA/CHIP conducted by a Catholic health care organization. See www.christushealth.org/about/donate/community-health/community-health-needs-assessment-and-implementation-plan. A detailed analysis of St. Vincent's efforts may be found in Kathy Armijo Etre, Dean Maines, and Paul J. Wojda, "CHRISTUS St. Vincent Hospital: Moving Beyond Random Acts of Kindness, Acting for the Common Good," presented at the Tenth International Conference on Catholic Social Thought in Business Education and the Sixth Colloquium on Christian Humanism in Business and Society, University of St. Thomas, St. Paul, MN, June 22, 2018.

Compared to Catholic health care organizations, very few Catholic universities are as deeply and as consistently "plugged in" to their surrounding communities, despite the ubiquity of university offices and community liaisons tasked with facilitating good relationships between "town and gown." The detachment of Catholic universities from their local communities, especially Catholic universities in densely urban settings, is often exacerbated by student populations that, for the most part, come from great distances away and neither know nor care much about their university's surrounding neighborhoods. Might Catholic health care ethicists help these students, academic moral theologians, and, thus, Catholic universities, develop more sophisticated and coordinated means of "plugging in" to their communities? It is not beyond the realm of possibility.

One obvious place to do this is the above-mentioned CHNA/CHIP process. In those contexts where the CHNA/CHIP process is well-conceived and established, Catholic health care organizations already partner with a range of external partners, including religious communities. Catholic colleges and universities, where curricular and extracurricular attention in matters related to health care, public health in particular, is already turning towards a focus on the "social determinants" of health, would simply be another such partner.

The prospect of collaboration with Catholic universities might be even more attractive for Catholic health care organizations looking to improve their community benefit processes but without the necessary institutional resources to do so. One potential beneficial consequence of thus connecting faculty and students in Catholic universities with mission leaders and health care ethicists in Catholic health care organizations would be to help further develop that "disciplined sensitivity to human suffering" that Michael Buckley has argued ought to be one of the aims of a Catholic university education. Catholic health care organizations might also find future mission leaders and health care ethicists among the students involved in the process. Of course, the communities served by both universities and health care organizations stand to benefit as well.

Finally, because Catholic health care ethicists tend to describe their work, and the work of Catholic health care organizations, as *ministries*, closer collaboration with them might also encourage academic moral theologians to consider their own work, and the work of Catholic universities, as *ministries*. In fact, *Ex Corde Ecclesiae* devotes five paragraphs to the topic of "pastoral ministry" and clearly sees it as an indispensable dimension of a Catholic university.

> Pastoral ministry is that activity of the University which offers the members of the university community an opportunity to integrate religious and moral principles with their academic study and non-aca-

demic activities, thus integrating faith with life. It is part of the mission of the Church within the University, and is also a constitutive element of a Catholic University itself, both in its structure and in its life. A university community concerned with promoting the Institution's Catholic character will be conscious of this pastoral dimension and sensitive to the ways in which it can have an influence on all university activities. (no. 38)

This passage maintains the crucial distinction between the properly academic and non-academic activities of a Catholic university, and subsequent paragraphs further reinforce the assumption that what constitutes "pastoral activity" in a Catholic university is largely confined to what goes on in offices of Campus Ministry or Student Life, not the library or the classroom. At the same time, however, pastoral ministry is also described as a *"constitutive element"* of a Catholic University, with a potentially pervasive influence "on all university activities." Thus, *Ex Corde Ecclesiae* at least implicitly expands the scope of ministry beyond those familiar boundaries. More formal collaboration with Catholic health care organizations could likely do the same, especially if that collaboration is understood as oriented toward the "reconciling" work of restoring community health, as it can be, for example, in the CHNA/CHIP process. Catholic universities might even begin thinking of themselves, as many Catholic health care organizations already do, as participating in the "healing ministry of Jesus." At any rate, Pope Francis's evocative metaphor of the church as "field hospital" makes it difficult to dismiss such conceptions out of hand.

None of which is to say that there is either clarity or consensus among those working in Catholic health care about what it means to describe their activities as a "ministry." Charles Bouchard has helpfully identified some of the ambiguities of the term "ministry" as it came into wider usage within Catholic health care over the last two decades.[28] Unfortunately, as he notes, "practice and language have gotten ahead of theology," and several questions need to be addressed if Catholic health care is to continue to claim the term. According to Bouchard, "there can be no meaningful appropriation of the term 'ministry' to describe Catholic health care [nor, we might add prospectively, Catholic higher education] unless it is nourished with serious theology and spirituality at a number of levels."[29] Here is precisely where ongoing dialogue with academic theologians dedicated to sustained inquiry on this very point could prove exceptionally fruitful.[30] It is a possibility that leads directly to our next question.

---

[28] Charles Bouchard, O.P., "Health Care as 'Ministry': Common Usage, Confused Theology," *Health Progress* 89, no. 3 (2008): 26-30.
[29] Bouchard, "Health Care as 'Ministry,'" 27-28.
[30] This dialogue is, in fact, already underway. See, for example, Thomas F. O'Meara, "Catholic Health Care's Ministry to the Future," in *Incarnate Grace: Perspectives on*

SHARED MINISTRY: THEOLOGICAL FOUNDATIONS

If academic moral theologians, and Catholic universities, can be said to benefit from closer collaboration with Catholic health care ethicists and the "healing ministry" of Catholic health care organizations, can the same be said in reverse? Can Catholic health care ethicists and Catholic health care organizations be said to benefit from closer collaboration with the *universitas magistrorum et scholarium* as envisioned by *Ex Corde Ecclesiae?* It might be argued, of course, that they already do benefit. To the extent Catholic health care ethicists have their degrees from Catholic universities, they are already members of that community of teachers and scholars, even if they are not on a specific university's payroll. In addition, Catholic health care ethicists benefit from opportunities for continuing education (e.g., conferences and workshops) and consulting services offered by the growing number of academic centers dedicated to health care ethics at Catholic universities, some with affiliated medical schools and some without.[31]

Substantively, however, the chief benefit of closer collaboration with academic moral theologians for Catholic health care ethicists will or at least *should* be the opportunity to participate in the ongoing effort to articulate more adequately the theological grounds of Catholic health care ethics, which will also include, if closer collaboration ensues, the theological grounds of that collaboration itself. An enormous amount of theological work has already been done, especially on the former point, and it is not the intention of this essay either to survey that work or to argue for the superiority of one theological account of Catholic health care ethics over another. However, given the ongoing challenges to both Catholic universities and Catholic health care organizations as described above, two points in particular merit further theological reflection. The first, which returns us to the "vocational" question of what it means and requires to be an academic moral theologian or Catholic health care ethicist, has to do with the concept of "participation," as it has been identified by Lisa Cahill in her account of "participatory" theological bioethics. The second point returns us to the "institutional" question of what it means and requires to be a Catholic university or Catholic health care organization, and the need for a more adequate "theology of institutions."

In *Theological Bioethics: Participation, Justice, Change,* Cahill rejects the common assumption that religiously grounded normative claims regarding questions of health and health care must, in a liberal

---

the Ministry of Catholic Health Care, ed. Charles Bouchard (St. Louis: The Catholic Health Association, 2017), 124-140.
[31] Kennedy Institute of Ethics at Georgetown, Albert Gnaegi Center for Health Care Ethics at Saint Louis University, Nieswanger Institute for Healthcare Ethics and Leadership at Loyola Chicago, Center for Health Policy and Ethics at Creighton, etc.

society, accept a marginalized status, in deference to the dominant discourses of science, economics, and individualism. These dominant discourses are not as "thin" as some suppose, she argues, for their power to persuade draws upon a stock of images, stories, and practices so familiar to citizens of liberal societies that they "are no longer directly observed."[32] Theologians speaking out of religious traditions would do well to draw upon their own images, stories, and practices, and so "dislodge" these entrenched discourses. "Participatory theological bioethics," so conceived, will accordingly place as much if not more emphasis on action as on speech.

> Theological ethics in the participatory mode recognizes that its persuasive value derives only in part from its intellectual coherence. It derives in equal or greater measure from its power to allude to or induce a shared sphere of behavior, oriented by shared concerns and goals, and its power to constitute relations of empathy and interdependence among the "arguers." To name theological-ethical discourse as participatory discourse is to hold up as an explicit goal the creation of connective practices among interlocutors in order that shared social practices may be transformed in light of religiously inspired (though not necessarily tribalistic) visions and values.[33]

As a "major example of participatory theological bioethics," Cahill singles out the Catholic Health Association (CHA) and its work "uniting religious ideals, ethical analysis, political activism, and health care institutions and practices."[34] (Her list, interestingly enough, does not include Catholic universities, but there is no reason it couldn't or shouldn't.)

Cahill's proposal has obvious bearing on the issue of closer collaboration between academic moral theologians and Catholic health care ethicists. Such collaboration would clearly constitute another node in the network of "connective practices" among interlocutors who, in this case, are united by a shared set of "religiously inspired vision and values." If Cahill is correct, the work of both academic moral theologians and Catholic health care ethicists would be potentially much more persuasive. However, much more theological work remains to be done here, especially around the term "participation" itself. On Cahill's terms, that theological work cannot take place independently of the collaboration of those engaged in it. In other words, what "participation" means theologically will only be disclosed in the context of the conversation, debate, and activity of those mutually committed to that collaboration itself.

---

[32] Lisa Sowle Cahill, *Theological Bioethics: Participation, Justice, Change* (Washington, DC: Georgetown University Press, 2005), 27.
[33] Cahill, *Theological Bioethics*, 38.
[34] Cahill, *Theological Bioethics*, 82.

Which brings us to the second, "institutional" question. If there is to be closer collaboration between academic moral theologians and Catholic health care ethicists, a richer theological account of their respective institutions will be necessary. Why? Primarily because, as Richard Gaillardetz notes in a recent essay on a "Theology of Institutions," the Catholic tradition has always insisted on the inescapably institutional character by which divine grace is mediated in human experience, principally but not exclusively through the "institutional church" itself.

> It is through church institutions that the church continues the mission and ministry of Jesus in the world. This conviction that God wishes to manifest God's work of reconciliation and healing through a people and its institutions, provides the basis for the distinctive Catholic conviction that we can see the church itself as a kind of sacrament.[35]

As "church institutions," Catholic universities and Catholic health care organizations both participate in this sacramental mediation of divine love. Both are called to reflect, in their distinct and irreducible ways, God's redemptive, reconciling love of God's creation (2 Cor. 5:19). Both constitute, in Benedict XVI's phrase, two different instantiations of the "institutional path" of *caritas*, which should not be considered inferior to the "individual path" (*Caritas in Veritate*, no. 7). Unless academic theologians recognize some aspect of this sacramental character at work in Catholic health care organizations and unless Catholic health care ethicists recognize some aspect of this sacramental character at work in Catholic universities, truly fruitful collaboration will be difficult to establish or else very short-lived.

A MODEL

As noted at the outset of this essay, it would be tempting to justify closer collaboration between academic moral theologians and Catholic health care ethicists on pragmatic grounds: academic moral theologians are in danger of disappearing altogether, and the supply of Catholic health care ethicists (and mission leaders generally) is running dangerously low. Having considered the historical circumstances that gave rise to the two vocations, some reasons for thinking closer collaboration might be beneficial for both, and two fundamental theological issues that will deserve further examination if such closer collaboration is to occur, we can hopefully see the limitations of a purely pragmatic approach to the issue. That approach tends to leave untouched all the crucial questions, none more important than what *sort*

---

[35] Richard Gaillardetz, "Theology of Institutions," in *Incarnate Grace: Perspectives on the Ministry of Catholic Health Care*, ed. Charles Bouchard (St. Louis: Catholic Health Association, 2017), 260.

of academic moral theologian and Catholic health care ethicist ought we to want as a consequence of closer collaboration?

The fundamental premise of this essay has been that closer collaboration between academic moral theologians and Catholic health care ethicists is best grounded on: a) the mutual recognition by members of each vocation that he or she already participates, in varying respects and to varying degrees, in the institutional ministry of the other; and b) the shared conviction that further interaction might contribute to the ongoing enrichment of both Catholic universities and Catholic health care organizations. If such a premise is persuasive, the next question is where individuals with such dispositions might be found or how they might be formed. It is, naturally, an institutional question.

There are, of course, many possible answers to it. One model that might be adapted is that employed by the Alliance for Catholic Education (ACE) program founded at the University of Notre Dame in the early 1990s.[36] ACE was founded to help under-resourced Catholic primary and secondary schools by forming qualified and energetic young college graduates to serve as teachers and administrative leaders in those schools, much like the "Teach for America" program with which it is partially affiliated. Thus, the ACE program consists of an institutional partnership between Catholic universities (Notre Dame primarily, but also others) and a (growing) network of Catholic K-12 schools across the country. Students selected for the highly competitive program spend two intensive summers doing coursework on the Notre Dame campus in South Bend. During the intervening two academic years these students then teach in an under-resourced school. In addition to transmitting the skills necessary to teach K-12 students, the program also emphasizes, in what are perhaps the key ingredients to its success, the development of personal spirituality and life in community (students are placed in their teaching-assignments in groups of three or more). Each student graduates with an M.A. in education and is typically licensed to teach in the State of their school placement. Many students continue teaching in Catholic schools after graduation.

How might this program be adapted to help facilitate closer collaboration between academic moral theologians and Catholic health care ethicists? For their part, Catholic health care institutions would need either to expand or create internship opportunities for qualified *groups* of students. Living arrangements allowing for community life would also need to be established, and qualified persons found who would be entrusted with supervision and direction of both individuals and communities. Catholic universities, for their part, would need to either adapt or create intensive M.A. programs in Catholic health care ethics

---

[36] See Alliance for Catholic Education, "About ACE," ace.nd.edu/about/the-alliance-for-catholic-education.

(and perhaps in mission leadership), as well as establishing the structures that would permit reflective community life. Obviously, faculty at Catholic universities would need to help identify and recruit potential candidates for such a program of study.

An older generation of health care ethicists might recognize in the ACE model something like a concentrated version of the formation they received in seminary. Indeed, that is very much what ACE seeks to do. That style of education, as Lisa Cahill might say, was always participatory (even if overly tribal). Whether the souls of Catholic health care organizations and Catholic universities can be saved may depend on whether it, or something like it, succeeds. M

Catholic Bioethicists and Moral Theologians Drifting Apart?: A Sequela of Specialization and Professionalization

Becket Gremmels

CATHOLIC THEOLOGY HAS A LONG HISTORY with health care. The allegory of Christ as the Divine Healer evidences the strong relationship between the two fields. Regarding moral theology, Augustine's writings on suicide (*City of God*, I.22) and Thomas Aquinas' discussion of amputation (ST II-II, q. 65, a. 1) and the beginnings of the principle of totality are well known, and even Tertullian wrote on maternal-fetal conflict (*On the Soul*, 25). Yet the focus of practicing Catholic bioethicists and academic moral theologians seems to have drifted apart over the past several decades. This drift has led to a disconnect between the theoretical arguments and topical concerns of moral theology and the practical, real-world concerns that bioethicists face in their daily cases, consults, and conversations with clinicians and hospital administrators.

As a consequence, the focus of moral theologians often differs from the problems that bioethicists and clinicians face on a daily basis. Subsequently, the theological discussion of issues most commonly faced by bioethicists is smaller than other areas of theological concern in bioethics. In this paper, I argue three points. First, this disconnect has been caused by a number of factors, especially the increasing specialization and professionalization of bioethicists. Second, Catholic bioethicists and moral theologians would mutually benefit from a closer relationship. Finally, both groups could take several steps towards this end without substantial effort or increase in time or resources.

To be clear, I am not claiming there is a complete or even substantial divergence between the two fields. Many of my ethics colleagues who currently work within health care organizations have degrees in moral theology. Furthermore, a number of texts on Catholic bioethics have been published by moral theologians in the past decade.[1] Thus,

---

[1] Nicanor Pier Giorgio Austriaco, *Biomedicine and Beatitude: An Introduction to Catholic Bioethics* (Washington DC: The Catholic University of America Press, 2011). David DeCosse and Thomas Nairn, ed., *Conscience and Catholic Health Care: From Clinical Contexts to Government Mandates* (Maryknoll, NY: Orbis Books,

there is a good amount of interaction between moral theologians and bioethicists, and many theologians are doing significant work in bioethics. Yet the relationship between theologians and bioethicists could be stronger. This opportunity for improvement is where I focus my comments.

CAUSES OF THE DRIFT

I see six factors behind the divergence between academic theologians and practicing bioethicists. First, bioethics has become a separate field of study in and of itself with its own subspecialties. Hence, it may be the case that moral theologians are not writing in bioethics as much as they used to, but it is in part because many now consider themselves to be bioethicists rather than moral theologians. The field of Catholic bioethics draws as much from theology as it does from philosophy, sociology, law, medicine, nursing, chaplaincy, business operations, health care administration, and a host of other fields. Moral theology can also be interdisciplinary and draw from other fields, but it is still theology at its core. Bioethics, on the other hand, cannot be said to be any of these at its core. It truly has become a field in its own right rather than a subspecialty or application of other fields. The *Encyclopedia of Bioethics* defines the field as "the systematic study of the moral dimensions – including moral vision, decisions, conduct, and policies – of the life sciences and health care, employing a variety of ethical methodologies in an interdisciplinary setting."[2]

The field of bioethics is even developing subspecialties of its own. Some bioethicists specialize in public health ethics or pediatric ethics, while others focus on clinical ethics or research ethics.[3] In fact, some subspecialties even have certificates or degrees, for example a certificate in public health ethics or pediatric ethics, or a doctorate in nursing

---

2017). C. Ryan McCarthy, *What to Do with the Least of Our Brothers?: Finding Moral Solutions to the Problem of Endangered Embryos* (Charlotte: St. Benedict Press, 2015). David F. Kelly, Gerard Magill, and Henk ten Have, *Contemporary Catholic Health Care Ethics*, 2nd ed. (Washington DC: Georgetown University Press, 2013).

[2] Thomas Warren Reich, *Encyclopedia of Bioethics, First Edition* (New York: Macmillan, 1995), xxi.

[3] These are broad generalizations, but, for an example on clinical research see Ana Iltis, "Lay concepts in informed consent to biomedical research: The capacity to understand and appreciate risk," *Bioethics* 20, no. 4 (2006): 180-190; for an example on standardization of health care ethics, see Mark Repenshek, "Attempting to Establish Standards in Ethics Consultation for Catholic Health Care: Moving Beyond a Beta Group," *Health Care Ethics USA* 18, no. 1 (2010): 5-14; for an example on organ issues, see James DuBois, "Increasing rates of organ donation: exploring the Institute of Medicine's boldest recommendation," *Journal of Clinical Ethics* 20, no. 1 (2009): 13-22; and for an example on moral distress, see Mary Corley, "Nurse Moral Distress and Ethical Work Environment," *Nursing Ethics* 12, no. 4 (2005): 381-390.

ethics.[4] Thus, rather than bioethics being a subspecialty of moral theology, as some theologians might see it, bioethics is now a field in its own right with subspecialties of its own.

Second, and closely related to the first, there is a growing trend towards professionalization among bioethicists, especially those in health care. This leads bioethicists to turn more inward towards bioethics rather than outward towards other fields like moral theology. I believe this trend is a direct result of the fact that bioethics has become its own field. After all, if it is a separate area of study distinct from others, it is only natural that some people would specialize in it. Today, health care ethics consultation is mostly performed by physicians or hospital employees who volunteer their time to participate on an ethics committee. They often have no formal or extensive training in ethics or health care ethics.[5] Some systems have explored various structural models that employ a combination of volunteer consultants and full-time ethicists.[6]

Yet several authors have described the benefits of a full-time ethicist.[7] Due to concern for the quality of background and education of all consultants, full-time or volunteer, some groups have proposed certification programs for health care ethics consultation. The **American Society for Bioethics and Humanities** has even created its Healthcare Ethics Consultant-Certified Program.[8] As numerous studies have shown the positive impact of ethics consultation on operational met-

---

[4] Graduate Certificate in Public Health Ethics, University of Massachusetts Amherst, www.umass.edu/sphhs-online/programs/graduate-certificate-public-health-ethics. Pediatric Bioethics Certificate, Children's Mercy Center for Bioethics, www.childrensmercy.org/bioethics/certificate-program. PhD in Nursing Ethics, Duquesne University, www.duq.edu/academics/schools/nursing/graduate-programs/phd-in-nursing-ethics.

[5] Ellen Fox, Sarah Myers, and Robert Pearlman, "Ethics Consultation in United States Hospitals: A National Survey," *American Journal of Bioethics* 7, no. 2 (2007): 17.

[6] Matthew Kenney, "A System Approach to Proactive Ethics Integration," *National Catholic Bioethics Quarterly* 18, no. 1 (2018): 93-112. Courtenay Bruce, Jocelyn Lapointe, Peter Koch, Katarina Lee, and Savitri Fedson, "Building a Vibrant Clinical Ethics Consultation Service," *National Catholic Bioethics Quarterly* 18, no. 1 (2018): 29-38.

[7] Kate Payne, "Reflections on the Role of Ethicists in the Catholic Health Ministry," *Health Care Ethics USA* 18, no. 2 (2010): 25-27. Birgitta Sujdak Mackiewicz, "Essential Goals of Ethics Committees and the Role of Professional Ethicists," *National Catholic Bioethics Quarterly* 18, no. 1 (2018): 49-57.

[8] American Society for Bioethics and Humanities, "Healthcare Ethics Consultant-Certified Program," asbh.org/certification/hcec-certification. American Society for Bioethics and Humanities, "Benefits of Certification for Leadership in Healthcare Ethics Consulting," asbh.org/certification/hec-c-benefits-to-leadership.

rics, it seems possible that the number of full-time positions for ethicists will grow.[9] Today, more full-time positions are available in health care ethics than ever before.

To fill these positions, educational programs tailored to bioethics, health care ethics, and clinical ethics have sprung up. At least three Catholic universities offer a PhD in bioethics (sometimes titled health care ethics), two offer a practical doctorate (doctorate in bioethics or health care ethics), and numerous universities offer master's degrees.[10] Moreover, both Catholic and non-Catholic universities and health centers offer fellowships in clinical ethics. These programs certainly entail an academic component, but they are substantially geared toward the practical aspects of health care ethics consultation. As part of their training, ethics fellows participate in clinical rounds with care teams, observe clinical ethics consults with faculty members, and eventually take call and perform consults independently. They learn how to interact with clinicians, patients, and family members to provide real-time advice in a manner that is meaningful and helpful to those involved. Just as clinicians must learn to avoid medical jargon when speaking with patients, ethics fellows learn to avoid theological, philosophical, and moral jargon.

In my view, this tendency toward professionalization and use of full-time clinical ethicists has made those professional ethicists more likely to read, write, and publish in bioethics. The more they specialize in bioethics and subspecialties of bioethics, the more invested they are in that narrow subspecialty. Consequently, they are less likely to read or publish in moral theology journals, for instance, such as the one in which this article appears. Conversely, moral theologians often subspecialize in specific areas of application or on specific questions within moral theology. Thus, for both groups, learning enough about the other field to speak competently becomes a barrier to entering it. The path of least resistance is to write in the area they know best, and that is often what occurs.

Third, bioethicists are increasingly focusing on subspecialized areas rather than more fundamental questions of method or frameworks,

---

[9] Selena Au, Philippe Couillard, Amanda Roze des Ordons, Kirsten Fiest, Dianne Lorenzetti, and Nathalie Jette, "Outcomes of Ethics Consultations in Adult ICUs: A Systematic Review and Meta-Analysis," *Critical Care Medicine* 46, no. 5 (2018): 799-808.

[10] For examples, see these among others: Albert Gnaegi Center for Health Care Ethics, Saint Louis University, bioethics.slu.edu; Center for Healthcare Ethics, Duquesne University, www.duq.edu/academics/schools/liberal-arts/about-us/centers/center-for-healthcare-ethics; Neiswanger Institute for Bioethics & Healthcare Leadership, Loyola University Chicago, hsd.luc.edu/bioethics; Center for Health Policy and Ethics, Creighton University, www.creighton.edu/chpe; Catholic Clinical Ethics Master's Program and Certificate Program, Catholic University of America and Georgetown University, clinicalethics.georgetown.edu.

which creates obstacles for theologians to enter debates given the extra time and research needed to become familiar with a topic's details. Historically, prominent bioethicists and theologians often wrote on any and all topics. Many of the seminal works like those of William May, Kevin O'Rourke, Jean deBlois, and Benedict Ashley, Orville Griese, and others addressed a wide variety of topics from organ donation and feeding tubes to informed consent and ectopic pregnancy.[11] Secular bioethicists were similar, as evidenced by the writings of Tom Beauchamp and Jim Childress, Albert Jonsen, Mark Siegler, and William Winslade, and Robert Veatch.[12] They certainly wrote in more detail on specific topics, but they were, in a sense, bioethics generalists.

However, as the field has matured, the number of topics and specific issues that draw our attention has grown exponentially. Very few bioethicists are able to be generalists nowadays, in part because the need for bioethics work nowadays increasingly requires bioethics specialists. This seems to be the natural evolution of any new field of academic inquiry: the first few generations lay the foundation(s) and subsequent generations build on that foundation by filling in the gaps on narrower issues. The scholars mentioned above wrote much on methodology, frameworks, and approaches to bioethics. These debates are not settled (nor do I think they ever will be), but the bioethics conversation as a whole seems to have moved away from methodology and more towards application. The field appears to be transitioning from foundation-building to gap-filling. This is true both for Catholic bioethicists and secular bioethics.

The sheer volume of issues demanding scholarly attention requires more discussion of application; yet, perhaps, this transition is also occurring because the questions of methodology are less prominent. If the broader approaches and frameworks are well-sketched in the literature, they may not warrant as much discussion as their application. Regardless, the increased focus on specialization and application makes it all the harder for moral theologians to break into the fray. The more specialized a discussion is, the more technical knowledge one needs to enter it. The fact that this technical knowledge is often in a field far outside theology, such as medicine or biology, probably does not help attract moral theologians either. The reverse is also true. The

---

[11] William May, *Catholic Bioethics and the Gift of Human Life, Third Edition*. (Huntington: Our Sunday Visitor, 2013); Orville M. Griese, *Catholic Identity in Health Care: Principles and Practice* (Braintree: The Pope John Center, 1987); Benedict Ashley, Jean deBlois, and Kevin O'Rourke, *Health Care Ethics: A Catholic Theological Analysis, Fifth Edition* (Washington DC: Georgetown University Press, 2006).

[12] Tom Beauchamp and James Childress, *Principles of Biomedical Ethics* (New York: Oxford University Press, 2012); Albert Jonsen, Mark Siegler, and William Winslade, *Clinical Ethics: A Practical Approach to Ethical Decisions in Clinical Medicine* (New York: McGraw-Hill, 2015); Robert Veatch, *The Basics of Bioethics* (New York: Routledge, 2016).

more time that bioethicists must spend on a specialized topic, the less time they have to devote to broader questions of moral theology or even to specialized topics within moral theology itself besides bioethics.

Fourth, the skillsets required of moral theologians in academia and those of ethicists in health care are quite different. This difference makes it difficult for anyone to excel at both, thus posing a barrier to someone in either field making a substantial impact on the other. The fast-paced nature of modern health care makes it very difficult for an ethicist working at a hospital or health system to devote significant time to scholarly work, and it also makes it difficult for theologians to be aware of emerging issues in real time. Some ethicists do not have publication or academic work as part of their job description, giving them no dedicated time to publish. Publishing may even be actively discouraged in some roles. Others simply lack interest in publishing, finding the practical problems and projects in their job more intellectually satisfying than publication. Yet even if there is some slight allowance for scholarly writing, the focus on productivity and operationalizing ethics can monopolize an ethicist's time.

The speed at which conversations take place also is unlike anything encountered in academia. Academics often take months or years to parse out every permutation and detail involved in a concept before publishing or presenting on it, which is quite appropriate given the expectations of their role and the nature of their inquiry. This requires a unique skillset including patience and analytical skills that those in health care ethics may not have. In contrast, those in health care do not have the luxury of time, especially in the clinical setting. One is expected to have conversations on any topic and think through many levels of nuance with little if any time to prepare a definitive response, sometimes less than thirty minutes. In this timeframe, one must sift through extraneous information (and there is much of it), identify the relevant moral factors (it is not uncommon for a single consult to have three or four major issues), weigh various options (and usually generate new ones the care team, patient, and family have not considered), and make a recommendation. This also requires a unique skillset including quick-thinking and the ability to triage priorities that those in academia may not have.

This skillset is more similar to the pastoral skills employed by those who put moral theology into practice like parish priests or confessors than to the skills used by those in academia who teach, read, write, and present. In my opinion, the former skillset was not required or expected of ethicists before the focus on professionalization in bioethics, but now it is starting to be expected. This change in skillset expectations increases the drift between theologians and ethicists. These skillsets are so different that it is hard to acquire one once you have the other, and it is a rare person who is equally skilled in both. Even for those who have both, it is hard to have the time to do both.

Fifth, some in academia have an aversion to applied fields as they find them unscholarly or not rigorous enough to be worthy of serious attention. Several authors have pointed out this tendency, especially among analytical philosophers, to look down on applied ethics.[13] I admit that I felt this way while studying philosophy as an undergraduate before I really encountered bioethics. However, I have learned through experience the necessity of nuanced, technical, theological discussion for health care ministry today. To have such a discussion with clinical colleagues who are unversed and untrained in moral theology is a daunting challenge. It requires conveying the technical concepts the field of moral theology has developed over the centuries without using any of the terms, concepts, words, or language that accompany these concepts.

Sixth, it is possible many moral theologians are unaware of the need for more bioethicists in Catholic health care, the need for younger ethicists (or those from related fields wishing to start a second career) to fill positions, and the attractive salaries these positions carry. Catholic health systems and hospitals have great difficulty finding qualified ethicists to fill jobs. Anecdotally, my current position at CHRISTUS Health was vacant for almost two years, and my previous position was vacant for more than two years after I left. Thankfully, the Catholic Health Association has collected data that illustrates this problem through three surveys of ethicists working in Catholic health care.[14] Table 1 shows the age breakdown of the forty-seven ethicists who responded to the 2015 survey.[15] This is consistent with the 2009 survey that found 68.9 percent of ethicists were fifty or older.

---

[13] Tom L. Beauchamp, "On Eliminating the Distinction between Applied Ethics and Ethical Theory," *The Monist* 67, no. 4 (1984): 514-531; Lou Marinoff, *Philosophical Practice* (New York: Elsevier, 2001), 185-186; Martha Holstein and Phyllis B. Mitzen, *Ethics in Community Based Elder Care* (New York: Springer Publishing Company, 2001), 23, n. 6.

[14] Thomas Nairn, "Ethicists in a Quickly Changing Environment," *Health Progress* 96, no. 4 (2015): 72-74; Ron Hamel, "Ethicists in Catholic Health Care: Taking Another Look," *Health Care Ethics USA* 23, no. 1 (2015): 34-44; Ron Hamel, "A Critical Juncture," *Health Progress* 90, no 2. (2009): 12-22. The third survey occurred in early 2018 and has not yet been published.

[15] Hamel, "Ethicists in Catholic Health Care: Taking Another Look," 35.

Drifting Apart 29

Table 1

Age	Percentage
20-29	4.5%
30-39	18.2%
40-49	13.6%
50-59	25%
60-69	36.4%
> 70	2.3%

Given this age, it is unsurprising that 70.6% of the 2015 respondents said they plan to retire in the next 15 years, or by 2029 (the survey occurred in late 2014). Moreover, there is a disproportionately smaller percentage of ethicists in the lower age range, especially 20-29 years old. Thus, many will be retiring in the coming years, and there are not enough qualified younger ethicists to fill those positions.

Regarding salary, the 2015 survey breaks down responses into increments of $25,000 (Table 2).[16]

Table 2

Salary Range	Percent of Respondents
$50,001 to $75,000	8.8%
$75,001 to $100,000	20.6%
$100,001 to $125,000	14.7%
$125,001 to $150,000	8.8%
$150,001 to $175,000	8.8%
$175,001 to $200,000	8.8%
$200,001 to $225,000	11.8%
$225,001 to $250,000	5.9%
$250,001 to $275,000	2.9%
$300,001 to $325,000	2.9%
$425,001 to $450,000	2.9%
$450,000 and above	2.9%

The salaries are also stratified by the scope of ethicist's role. Unsurprisingly, those who work at an acute care facility fall between $75,000 and $175,000, those in a regional position range from $50,000 to $325,000, and those at the system level fall between $100,000 and $450,000 and above. These numbers are slightly higher than the 2009 survey. It is reasonable to conclude that more moral theologians would be interested in working in Catholic health care as ethicists if they

---

[16] Hamel, "Ethicists in Catholic Health Care: Taking Another Look," 37.

were familiar with this data on demographics and salaries. This seems especially true since most moral theologians already have the educational background of many ethicists. In the 2015 survey, 63.6 percent held a PhD in philosophy, moral theology, or a related field.

BENEFITS OF INTERACTION

These six reasons have led moral theologians and bioethicists in Catholic health care to drift apart over the past few decades (and it is certainly possible that there are other reasons I have not mentioned here). There are at least three benefits for increased interaction between moral theologians and Catholic ethicists. First, ethicists would benefit from more work by moral theologians on practical topics they frequently encounter. If the two groups do not interact then they do not communicate. If they do not communicate, then they cannot listen to each other. If they do not listen, they cannot encounter ideas relevant to their work. This leads to a lack of familiarity among theologians with the moral issues that Catholic health care actually faces, which in turn leads to a lack of scholarly interest. Moral theologians sometimes write on topics that have substantive theological implications but are rarely encountered by health care ethicists. Human embryonic stem cell research is a good example of this. Dozens of conference presentations, articles, and even entire books have been devoted to this topic. Certainly, it is a fascinating moral issue, serious and worthy of discussion, but one I rarely encounter. In over one thousand ethics consults I have performed so far in my career, I have had only four or five that were related to stem cell research. Even then, the consults centered more on the question of morally justified cooperation than on stem cell research specifically.

Yet ethicists in Catholic health care regularly encounter other topics which warrant deeper theological discussion, such as medically inappropriate treatment (or its misnomer medical futility). This topic touches on Church teaching on proportionate and disproportionate means but is also related to moral distress, burnout of clinicians, respect for human dignity and just distribution of resources. Other issues include shared decision making, informed assent for minors, the limits of the obligation to provide charity care, just distribution of resources in a disaster or decision making capacity. By applying their unique skillset to these topics, moral theologians could make a lasting impact on the provision of health care.

Second, stronger engagement in bioethics from theologians could have an influence not just on Catholic bioethics but secular bioethics as well. The smaller proportion of theologians prominently engaging in secular bioethics has led secular ethicists to overlook the contributions theologians have made to these debates. This oversight is both historical and contemporary, as seen in a recent issue of the *American*

Journal of Bioethics, a prominent secular bioethics journal. In the target article, the authors casually claim that the pioneers of bioethics "were almost to a person ethics or humanism professors."[17] Granted, the authors' list of pioneers includes three Catholic and two non-Catholic theologians, yet the first "pioneer" ironically began his career in 1971, which is the same year the second edition of the *Ethical and Religious Directives for Catholic Health Care Facilities* was published by the National Conference of Catholic Bishops. While this was officially the second edition, it was, arguably, the fourth edition.[18] Catholic moral theologians and ethicists in the United States had been working in bioethics (or medical ethics) for decades before the first pioneers on this list, yet none are mentioned by the authors.

Similarly, a response to this article in the same issue is titled, "Where Have All the Theologians Gone and Should We Lament Their Passing?"[19] The authors note that some theologians still work in bioethics but mostly in academia and that the majority of those doing health care ethics consults nowadays do not have any formal training in theology. They lament this change and argue the field of bioethics is weakened by this lack of diversity. While this claim is similar to my own here, that there has been a decrease in the percentage of theologians among those who work in bioethics (especially clinical ethics), it neglects the ethicists and ethics consultants in the 654 Catholic hospitals throughout the United States.[20] It is worth noting that this oversight of the historical and contemporary contribution of theologians is relatively new. In his book *The Birth of Bioethics*, published in 1998, Albert Jonsen devotes an entire chapter to the contributions of theologians to bioethics in the 1960s and 1970s.[21] Jonsen also notes the significant work in medical ethics done by moral theologians over the past few centuries, especially in the late nineteenth and early twentieth centuries.[22] It is discomforting to know they see bioethics as a secular field dominated by secular thinkers and even more discomforting to know that they are likely correct. Catholic bioethics and moral theology has much to offer secular bioethics due to the origin and content

---

[17] Bruce White, Wayne Shelton, and Cassandra Rivais, "Were the 'Pioneer' Clinical Ethics Consultants 'Outsiders'? For Them, Was 'Critical Distance' That Critical?" *American Journal of Bioethics*, 18, no. 6 (2018): 34-44.
[18] Kevin O'Rourke, Thomas Kopfensteiner, and Ron Hamel, "A Brief History: A Summary of the Development of the Ethical and Religious Directives for Catholic Health Care Services," *Health Progress* 82, no. 6 (2001): 18-21.
[19] Cynthia Geppert and Toby Schonfeld, "Where Have All the Theologians Gone and Should We Lament Their Passing?" *American Journal of Bioethics* 18, no. 6 (2018): 60-62.
[20] Catholic Health Association, "Facts and Statistics," www.chausa.org/about/about/facts-statistics.
[21] Albert Jonsen, *The Birth of Bioethics* (New York: Oxford University Press, 1998).
[22] Jonsen. *The Birth of Bioethics,* 35-37.

of its thought. An increase in the presence of moral theologians writing in secular bioethics or working in health care ethics could get more exposure for their ideas.

Third, a closer relationship between Catholic bioethicists and moral theologians would connect academic investigation with daily lived experience and practical ethicists with elements of the broader theological tradition. New practical approaches could arise from theoretical discussions, and new insights into theological concepts could stem from solutions to practical problems. Several recent works have such implications. To the first, Martin Rhonheimer's book on maternal-fetal conflict re-examines the reasons underlying why killing is wrong and what distinguishes the justified, indirect causing of death and the intentional, purposeful taking of human life.[23] His insights provide a new way of responding to cases of ectopic pregnancy and, by extrapolation, any situation in which a pregnancy threatens the life of a woman.

Regarding new insights into theory, in analyzing Physician Orders for Life Sustaining Treatment (POLST) forms, Peter Cataldo and Elliott Bedford make some important contributions to the broader theoretical discussion of proportionate and disproportionate means. They state that, when determining whether a particular treatment is proportionate or disproportionate:

> Catholic moral teaching and tradition have never limited the determination of what is ethically proportionate treatment to the immediate, present-moment circumstances. The evaluation of circumstances is inclusive of both circumstances in the present moment and circumstances that may reasonably be foreseen in the future.[24]

This point is an important distinction in the discussion regarding POLST forms and, to my knowledge, is not addressed in magisterial teaching or the Catholic moral tradition.

Other authors make another important theoretical point regarding the application of the principle of double effect to maternal-fetal vital conflict. Much of the discussion regarding double effect and abortion over the past century has focused on the good effect as the cure of a pathological condition of the pregnant woman. The authors point out the principle of double effect itself does not require a pathology be cured, merely that a good effect be achieved. They posit that "intervening to eliminate the threat to a person's life, even if it does not

---

[23] Martin Rhonheimer. *Vital Conflicts in Medical Ethics: A Virtue Approach to Craniotomy and Tubal Pregnancies* (Washington, DC: Catholic University of America Press, 2009).
[24] Peter Cataldo and Elliott Bedford, "Prospective Medical-Moral Decision Making," *National Catholic Bioethics Quarterly* 15, no. 1 (2015): 60.

eliminate a persistent underlying pathological condition, can be sufficient to satisfy the moral criteria" involved.[25] These are but two examples, and there are many others. Whether one agrees with the practical application used in these articles or not, the theoretical points these authors make are relevant to the broader moral tradition. Despite the move from generalist bioethics to specialized topics described above, bioethics literature can offer new insights into the foundational concepts of moral theology. By following that literature closely, moral theologians could also add to the theory and development of bioethics and moral theology in ways bioethicists cannot.

PROPOSING A RAPPROCHEMENT

While much could be done to strengthen the relationship between ethicists in Catholic health care and moral theologians, four possible steps stand out. First, moral theologians in the academy writing in medical ethics could seek out a local hospital, volunteer to be on their ethics committee, or even serve as a liaison or dialogue partner for their ethicist if they have one. If there is no Catholic hospital nearby, theologians could seek out non-Catholic hospitals. Every hospital accredited by The Joint Commission (TJC) must have a mechanism to address ethical issues that arise in patient care. Since TJC accredits 88% of accredited hospitals in the United States, it would not be difficult to find a local hospital interested in a moral theologian's expertise.[26]

Second, moral theologians and Catholic bioethicists could be more visible in each other's fields of study. For moral theologians, this includes publishing in Catholic bioethics journals like *Christian Bioethics*, *Health Care Ethics USA*, *Health Progress*, *The Linacre Quarterly*, *National Catholic Bioethics Quarterly*, or even secular bioethics journals like *American Journal of Bioethics*, *Cambridge Quarterly of Healthcare Ethics*, the *Hastings Center Report*, *Healthcare Ethics Committee (HEC) Forum*, or *Journal of Clinical Ethics*, to name a few. Similarly, they should consider attending bioethics conferences like the Catholic Medical Association, American Society of Bioethics and Humanities, the International Conference on Clinical Ethics Consultation, or the Pediatric Bioethics Conference at Seattle Children's, to name a few. The *American Journal of Bioethics* maintains and updates a list of secular bioethics events.[27]

---

[25] Ascension Health Colloquium, "Medical Interventions in Cases of Maternal-Fetal Vital Conflicts: A Consensus Statement," *National Catholic Bioethics Quarterly* 14, no. 3 (2014): 487.
[26] The Joint Commission, "Facts About Hospital Accreditation," www.jointcommission.org/facts_about_hospital_accreditation.
[27] bioethics.net, "Bioethics Events," www.bioethics.net/events.

On the other hand, ethicists in Catholic health care could follow theology journals just as they follow those in bioethics, medicine, nursing, and business. They stand to gain insight from their moral theology colleagues. Their discussions are bound to open new avenues of thought and investigation that they would not discover on their own. If they do not read moral theology, they cannot benefit from the expertise of moral theologians. Similarly, attending theology conferences like the Catholic Theological Society of America would allow ethicists to engage with theologians first hand. Submitting talks to conferences like this would get the concerns of Catholic bioethicists even more direct exposure to academics.

Third, ethicists in Catholic health care could contribute more to the literature as a whole. Many ethicists in Catholic health care do not publish regularly, so even one publication a year in a bioethics or theology journal would be a significant advancement. I suggest a standard of at least one article, essay, or letter to the editor per year. Ethicists could also include scholarly publication as part of their job description. For those ethicists who write multiple articles per year, consider submitting one per year to a journal that is more strictly theology than bioethics. Opening discussions in these venues on topics of concern to ethicists in Catholic health care would go a long way to benefitting from the reflective insight of moral theologians. While it is important to focus on these practical issues, it is just as important to consider them in a reflective manner removed from time constraints and potential conflicts of interest, which is traditionally the role of moral theologians.

Fourth, ethicists could consider occasionally teaching at a local Catholic university, perhaps even obtaining an adjunct position, even if it is for only one class a year. This could be in the theology department, but even philosophy or health sciences would be beneficial. If it is impractical to add this to the time commitments of modern health care, offer to be a guest lecturer for a class once a semester. It provides positive exposure for the health system and could prompt students to consider a career in Catholic health care as a bioethicist, mission leader, chaplain, or even a clinician. Alternatively, universities and health systems could work together to create non-traditional positions. For example, they could design two full-time positions in which each person spends half their time at each institution, or a teaching assistantship funded by both institutions that functions as an intern or fellow at the health system. This is likely the most difficult of these steps, but expanding any of these options would go far in bringing moral theologians and ethicists in Catholic health care closer together.

OBLIGATION TO WORK TOGETHER
While it may be true that moral theology and Catholic bioethics have drifted apart, they have not completely diverged. This drifting

seems to be a natural consequence of the professionalization of bioethics as its own field, the specialization of ethicists in different areas of bioethics, the different skillsets required by academia and the health care, an aversion among some academics to applied theology, and a lack of knowledge among moral theologians about basic demographics of Catholic ethicists. Bringing Catholic bioethicists and theologians closer together would enrich both fields (and maybe secular bioethics as well). For bioethicists, this would provide access to more analytical deep thought on the practical troubles they face daily. For moral theologians, this would be one more way they can further develop a living theology attentive to the needs of the flock and to answer Pope Francis's call to "be shepherds, with the 'odour of the sheep', make it real, as shepherds among your flock, fishers of men."[28] As representatives of the largest united provider of health care in the world, moral theologians and Catholic bioethicists have an obligation to work collaboratively to smell like sheep together. **M**

---

[28] Pope Francis, "Chrism Mass Homily," March 28, 2013, w2.vatican.va/content/francesco/en/homilies/2013/documents/papa-francesco_20130328_messa-crismale.html.

Equally Strange Fruit: Catholic Health Care and the Appropriation of Residential Segregation

Cory D. Mitchell and M. Therese Lysaught

It is necessary, therefore, for the privileged and the underprivileged to work on the common environment for the purpose of providing normal experiences of fellowship. This is one very important reason for the insistence that segregation is a complete ethical and moral evil.[1]

The penalty of deception is to become a deception, with all sense of moral discrimination vitiated.[2]
~Howard Thurman

FROM THE EARLIEST BEGINNINGS OF CHRISTIAN history and from the moment the Ursuline Sisters opened the first Catholic hospital in the United States in 1728, charity toward the poor and marginalized has been the chief identifying characteristic of Catholic health care.[3] Again and again, small groups of intrepid nuns sought out the poorest communities, set up hospitals, innovated on reimbursement methods, raised donations, lived in solidarity with and dedicated their lives to caring for the health needs of the poor, needs often exacerbated by extraordinarily difficult living conditions.[4]

Those Sisters would scarcely recognize Catholic health care today. In the second half of the twentieth century, United States health care delivery and payment systems underwent significant developments. Via ongoing consolidation and intense focus on the bottom line by highly trained management executives and corporate boards, Catholic

---

[1] Howard Thurman, *Jesus and the Disinherited* (Boston: Beacon Press, 1976), 88.
[2] Thurman, *Jesus*, 55.
[3] For the most comprehensive history of Catholic health care in the U.S., see Christopher J. Kauffman, *Ministry and Meaning: A Religious History of Catholic Health Care in the United States* (New York: Crossroads Press, 1995).
[4] For the vibrant stories of these founding Sisters, see Suzy Farren, *A Call to Care: The Women Who Built Catholic Healthcare in America* (St. Louis: Catholic Health Association, 1996).

health systems have evolved into multi-billion-dollar corporations.[5] In 2016, the four largest systems in the country had combined revenues of nearly $67 billion.[6] Catholic health care has become an economic powerhouse, certainly the most profitable ministry in the history of the church.

Yet these astounding revenues have been generated within a system rife with structural injustices. One of these has been the *de facto* residential segregation and rapid black community disinvestment in the U.S. in the late twentieth century.[7] Scholars have documented how intentional legislative and economic practices, amplified by tacit social dynamics, created urban pockets of concentrated poverty.[8] Such neighborhoods damage health in myriad ways. As Paul Farmer has famously noted, "diseases themselves make a preferential option for the poor."[9] Not only is residential segregation a fundamental cause of health disparities between blacks and whites, sicker patients require more care; consequently, those living in segregated communities find themselves also disproportionately burdened by health care costs.

Thus, residential segregation, as configured in the U.S., inflicts increased morbidity and mortality on human persons and undermines human flourishing in a variety of ways. As such, a case could be made that residential segregation constitutes an intrinsic evil.[10] Ordinarily, discussion of intrinsic evils in Catholic health care limits itself to abortion, tubal ligations, and physician assisted suicide. Yet, as John Paul

---

[5] Barbra Mann Wall, *American Catholic Hospitals: A Century of Changing Markets and Missions* (New Brunswick: Rutgers University Press, 2011).
[6] Laura Dyrda, "10 Largest US Health Systems: Which Had the Biggest Revenue Increase in 2016?" *Becker's Hospital Review*, March 3, 2017, www.beckershospitalreview.com/hospital-finance/10-largest-us-health-systems-which-had-the-biggest-revenue-increase-in-2016.html.
[7] In this article, we use the term "residential segregation" to encompass both racial segregation as well as the concentrated poverty or economic segregation with which it is currently inextricably intertwined in the United States. While thriving African-American communities are possible, such communities generally are often mixed-income communities and require external investment and intentionality on the part of residents and allies. They also presume the wider global context of oppression of black persons (as does even the mythical Wakanda in the film *Black Panther*). More specifically, residential segregation is a product of white housing policy and practice rather than a function of black preference (see footnote 8).
[8] Douglas S. Massey and Nancy Denton, *American Apartheid: Segregation and the Making of the Underclass* (Cambridge: Harvard University Press, 1993). See also David Hilfiker, *Urban Injustice: How Ghettos Happen* (New York: Seven Stories Press, 2003).
[9] Paul Farmer, "Medicine and Social Justice," *America*, July 15, 1995, 13-17.
[10] The evidence for this is supplied in part I below. We bracket the question of whether the category of intrinsic evil remains theologically tenable; we draw on it here insofar as it remains an operative category in Catholic moral theology, particularly within the *Ethical and Religious Directives for Catholic Health Care Services*.

II notes in *Veritatis Splendor*, the concept encompasses a much broader array of realities:

> The Second Vatican Council itself, in discussing the respect due to the human person, gives a number of examples of such acts [which, in the Church's moral tradition, have been termed " intrinsically evil" (*intrinsece malum*)]: " Whatever is hostile to life itself, such as any kind of homicide, genocide, abortion, euthanasia and voluntary suicide; whatever violates the integrity of the human person, such as mutilation, physical and mental torture and attempts to coerce the spirit; whatever is offensive to human dignity, such as *subhuman living conditions*, arbitrary imprisonment, deportation, *slavery*, prostitution and trafficking in women and children; degrading conditions of work which treat labourers as mere instruments of profit, and not as free responsible persons: all these and the like are a disgrace, and so long as they infect human civilization they contaminate those who inflict them more than those who suffer injustice, and they are a negation of the honour due to the Creator" (no. 80).[11]

African-American residential segregation in the United States is a ubiquitous vestige of slavery, and black ghettos certainly constitute subhuman living conditions. They are hostile to life itself; they violate the integrity of the human persons who live within them; and they are offensive to human dignity. Residentially segregated neighborhoods are therefore, as the pope continues, "by their very nature 'incapable of being ordered' to God, because they radically contradict the good of the person made in his image...they are such *always and per se* [evil]; in other words, on account of their very object, and quite apart from the ulterior intentions of the one acting and the circumstances" (no. 80).

Catholic health care publicly opposes discrimination. Many Catholic hospitals have signed the "Pledge to Act to Eliminate Health Care Disparities."[12] The U.S. Bishops open the *Ethical and Religious Directives for Catholic Health Care Services* (ERDs) with a vision of "The Social Responsibility of Catholic Health Care Services" noting:

> Catholic health care should distinguish itself by service to and advocacy for those people whose social condition puts them at the margins of our society and makes them particularly vulnerable to discrimination: the poor; the uninsured and the underinsured; children and the unborn; single parents; the elderly; those with incurable diseases and

---

[11] Emphasis added. See also *Gaudium et Spes*, no. 27.
[12] Julie Minda, "Catholic Providers Pledge to Address Race, Class-Based Inequity in Health Care," *Catholic Health World* 32, no. 7 (2016): www.chausa.org/publications/catholic-health-world/archives/issues/april-15-2016/catholic-providers-pledge-to-address-race-class-based-inequity-in-health-care.

chemical dependencies; racial minorities; immigrants and refugees (no. 3).

This is certainly a who's-who of those in residentially-segregated neighborhoods.

Yet is there a shadow side? While the Catholic church provides a powerful public voice against abortion as an intrinsic evil, it remains painfully silent on the omnipresence of residential segregation. While Catholic health care draws a bright line around abortion and contraception, refusing to participate in them or benefit from them financially, is Catholic health care tacitly and perhaps unknowingly enmeshed in residential segregation, perhaps even benefiting from or perpetuating it? Providing health care to persons in poor communities is good, but the excess morbidity and mortality borne by African Americans due to residential segregation imposes upon them disproportionate health care expenditures, expenditures which flow into and thereby benefit care providers. If such care simply attends to symptoms produced by residential segregation, accruing financial benefits from it without curing the cause, we must ask whether Catholic health care participates in residential segregation in a way that is ethically problematic.

Certainly, Catholic health care does not will the evil of residential segregation. When faced with involvement in an evil one does not will, traditional moral theology turns to the concept of moral cooperation. M. Cathleen Kaveny provides an alternative tool for looking at this question, namely, what she calls "a new category of appropriation of evil."[13] Following Kaveny, in this paper we ask: are there ways that Catholic health care *appropriates* the evil of residential segregation? Kaveny's analysis largely confines itself to traditional clinical questions considered within Catholic bioethics. We argue that her category is equally and perhaps more powerfully applicable at the interface of Catholic bioethics and social questions.

In what follows, we begin by detailing the myriad ways that residential segregation drives health disparities, using cardiovascular disease as a lens. We then point to subtle ways that such segregation benefits United States health care. Next, displaying Kaveny's category of appropriation of evil—and its concepts of moral seepage, self-deception, and ratification—we bring into visibility ways that Catholic health care institutions may materially appropriate the evils of subhuman living conditions. It also enables us to surface and develop implicit dimensions of Kaveny's framework, concepts we name moral inhibition, scandal, and implicit ratification. We close by suggesting

---

[13] M. Cathleen Kaveny, "Appropriation of Evil: Cooperation's Mirror Image," *Theological Studies* 61, no. 2 (2000): 280-313.

remedies for such appropriation—moving from charity care and community benefit to community building—which enable Catholic health care to deploy tools already at their disposal to focus on *structural* or environmental determinants of health.[14] In so doing, Catholic health care can not only bandage the wounds inflicted by residential segregation; it can begin to partner to dismantle it.

RESIDENTIAL SEGREGATION AS A DRIVER OF HEALTH DISPARITIES

Residential segregation is a fundamental reality for many African Americans. In 1990, slightly more than 45 percent of all African Americans lived in ghettos.[15] Ghettos are herein defined as neighborhoods or census tracts of concentrated poverty where incomes for upwards of 40 percent of households fall below the federal poverty level. The federal poverty threshold for a family of two adults and one child was $10,520 in 1990. Over the next three decades, this figure doubled to $20,420, while the demographics became even more dire, with more than 60 percent of African Americans living in metropolitan statistical areas of moderate to high poverty and segregation.[16]

Such concentrated poverty impairs health both directly through biopsychosocial pathways and indirectly through the lack of goods and services necessary to maintain healthy living. Indirect effects—such as loss of medical infrastructure, lack of helpful public services, and inadequate allocation of goods and services—are widely recognized.[17] Residential segregation concerns more than just housing; rather, it comprises a multi-dimensional assault. As Khaleeq Lutfi et al. note, "concentrated poverty is associated with the loss of resources out of a neighborhood resulting in the deterioration of neighborhood quality. These resources include quality medical care, quality education, and

---

[14] Social and structural determinants alone account for about 50 percent of health status, while health behaviors account for 30% and clinical care alone for 20 percent. Bridget Booske, Jessica C. Athens, David K. Kindig, and Patrick L.A. Remington, "Different Perspectives for Assigning Weights to Determinants of Health," *County Health Rankings Working Paper*, www.countyhealthrankings.org/sites/default/files/differentPerspectivesForAssigningWeightsToDeterminantsOfHealth.pdf.

[15] Paul A. Jargowsky, "Ghetto Poverty among Blacks in the 1980s," *Journal of Policy Analysis & Management* 13, no. 2 (1994): 288-310.

[16] For data on the federal poverty level, see U.S. Department of Health and Human Services, aspe.hhs.gov/prior-hhs-poverty-guidelines-and-federal-register-references.

[17] David R. Williams and Chiquita Collins, "Racial Residential Segregation: A Fundamental Cause of Racial Disparities in Health," *Public Health Reports* 116, no. 5 (2001): 404-416. See also Irma Corral, Hope Landrine, Yongping Hao, Luhua Zhao, Jenelle L. Mellerson, and Dexter L. Cooper, "Residential Segregation, Health Behavior and Overweight/Obesity among a National Sample of African-American Adults," *Journal of Health Psychology* 17, no. 3 (2012): 371-378.

Equally Strange Fruit 41

employment opportunities."[18] In addition, the economic disinvestment concurrent with the process of ghettoization increases unemployment and results in poor education, delinquency, crime, and the physical decay of buildings and infrastructure.[19]

Yet direct impacts of ghetto infrastructure on residents' health plays a more significant role. In a literature review, Harvard social epidemiologist David Williams and sociologist Chiquita Collins concluded that residential segregation is a fundamental cause of black-white health disparities.[20] They note that disparities in deaths from coronary heart disease and infant mortality have grown since 1950 despite advances in biomedicine and technology. According to the Institute of Medicine, disparities persist even when variables like insurance, individual-level income, and condition acuity are comparable.[21] For example, infant mortality rates among African Americans should disturb every institution concerned about the sanctity of life. For every 0.1 point change (on a scale of 0 to 1) in residential segregation as measured by a dissimilarity index, which measures how much census tracts deviate from complete desegregation, we see a one percent increase in pre-term birth rates and low birth weight; both are risk factors for infant mortality.[22]

While insurance, individual-level income and illness acuity may have small impacts on health disparities, neighborhoods exert a tremendous influence on health.[23] Well-established racial disparities in cardiovascular disease (CVD) provide a useful example to frame our

---

[18] Khaleeq Lutfi, Mary Jo Trepka, Kristopher P. Fennie, Gladys Ibanez, and Hugh Gladwin, "Racial Residential Segregation and Risky Sexual Behavior among Non-Hispanic Blacks, 2006–2010," *Social Science & Medicine* 140 (2015): 95-103.

[19] Gregory Brown, James Vigil, and Eric Taylor, "The Ghettoization of Blacks in Los Angeles: The Emergence of Street Gangs," *Journal of African-American Studies* 16, no. 2 (2012): 209-225.

[20] Williams and Collins, "Racial Residential Segregation," 404-416.

[21] Alan Nelson, "Unequal Treatment: Confronting Racial and Ethnic Disparities in Health Care," *Journal of the National Medical Association* 94, no. 8 (2002): www.ncbi.nlm.nih.gov/pmc/articles/PMC2594273/.

[22] Kwame Nyarko and George Wehby, "Residential Segregation and the Health of African-American Infants: Does the Effect Vary by Prevalence?" *Maternal and Child Health Journal* 16, no. 7 (2012): 1491-1499.

[23] Individual-level socioeconomic status (SES) contributes to CVD disparities. Using the National Health and Nutrition Examination Survey (NHANES), Kanjilal et al. found that while the prevalence of high blood pressure decreased from 1971-2002 for all four of their data-derived income groups—and the steepest decline was in the lowest income group—the prevalence for those in the lowest SES quartile was significantly higher than for those in the highest quartile (S. Kanjilal, E.W. Gregg, Y.J. Cheng, P. Zhang, D.E. Nelson, G. Mensah, and G.L. Beckles. "Socioeconomic Status and Trends in Disparities in 4 Major Risk Factors for Cardiovascular Disease among US Adults, 1971-2002," *Archives of Internal Medicine* 166, no. 21 (2006): 2348-55). See also I. Grotto, M. Huerta, and Y. Sharabi, "Hypertension and Socioeconomic Status," *Current Opinion in Cardiology* 23, no. 4 (2008): 335-339.

discussion. African Americans are 40 percent more likely than their white counterparts to have high blood pressure,[24] higher heart rates,[25] and higher age-adjusted heart disease death rates (30 percent higher for black men and 40 percent higher for black women).[26] Thus, blacks are at increased risk for CVD morbidity and mortality.

Like infant mortality, CVD prevalence and risk factors are more strongly correlated with neighborhood characteristics. In Harlem, New York, a study of 2,846 death certificates spanning a three-year period (1979-1981) found CVD-related deaths to constitute the majority of excess mortality rates.[27] Likewise, Major and colleagues prospectively analyzed 33,831deaths in 18,603 census-tract derived neighborhoods in six states from 1995 to 2005.[28] CVD mortality risks were elevated by 33 percent for men and 18 percent for women living in the most deprived neighborhoods. A study of coronary heart disease incidence examined 13,009 participants from 595 census block groups for a maximum follow-up period of 11.1 years.[29] Even after adjusting for individual-level income, education, and occupation, the risk of incident coronary heart disease increased three-fold for whites living in the most deprived neighborhoods compared to those in the most advantaged neighborhoods and 2.5 times for blacks. Significantly, those living in neighborhoods of concentrated poverty are at increased risk of developing CVD *regardless of race.*

What about neighborhood disadvantage is so dangerous for health? Evidence points to the psychosocial stress correlated with residential

---

[24] National Center for Health Statistics, "Health, United States," in *Health, United States, 2011: With Special Feature on Socioeconomic Status and Health* (Hyattsville: National Center for Health Statistics, 2012); and F.L. Brancati, W.H. Kao, A.R. Folsom, R.L. Watson, and M. Szklo, "Incident Type 2 Diabetes Mellitus in African-American and White Adults: The Atherosclerosis Risk in Communities Study," *Journal of the American Medical Association* 283, no. 17 (2000): 2253-2259.
[25] J.J. McGrath, K.A. Matthews, and S.S. Brady, "Individual Versus Neighborhood Socioeconomic Status and Race as Predictors of Adolescent Ambulatory Blood Pressure and Heart Rate," *Social Science and Medicine* 63, no. 6 (2006): 1442-1453.
[26] K.D. Kochanek, J. Xu, S.L. Murphy, A.M. Miniño, and H.C. Kung, "Deaths: Final Data for 2009," *National Vital Statistics Reports* 60, no. 3 (2011): 1-116.
[27] Collin McCord and Harold P. Freeman, "Excess Mortality in Harlem," *New England Journal of Medicine* 322, no. 3 (1990): 173-177.
[28] Jacqueline M. Major, Chyke A. Doubeni, Neal D. Freedman, Yikyung Park, Min Lian, Albert R. Hollenbeck, Arthur Schatzkin, Barry I. Graubard, and Rashmi Sinha et al., "Neighborhood Socioeconomic Deprivation and Mortality: Nih-Aarp Diet and Health Study," *PLoS One* 5, no. 11 (2010): e15538.
[29] A.V. Diez Roux, S.S. Merkin, D. Arnett, L. Chambless, M. Massing, F.J. Nieto, P. Sorlie, M. Szklo, H.A. Tyroler, R.L. Watson, "Neighborhood of Residence and Incidence of Coronary Heart Disease," *New England Journal of Medicine* 345, no. 2 (2001): 99-106.

segregation as the primary etiology.[30] Across the United States, central city ghettos are typically the oldest and most deteriorated portion of a metropolitan area. Such environmental cues can generate a fear of real or perceived crime resulting in chronic stress and increased blood pressure.[31] In fact, simply greening a few blighted or vacant lots in a neighborhood can decrease heart rate and blood pressure.[32]

Three studies are helpful here. First, Ross and Mirowsky posited a theoretical model in which neighborhood disadvantage drove neighborhood-level physical and social disorder, which in turn drove individual fear and concomitantly inhibited walking, which ultimately impacted health.[33] Fear was hypothesized to over-activate the fight-or-flight stress response, which can cause increased blood pressure, heart

---

[30] The racial-genetic model and the behavioral model seek to locate the cause of disparities primarily or solely in flawed individuals rather than flawed social systems. While such factors play a role in health status, research substantiates that neither is sufficient to account for the magnitude of health disparities. See C.W. Kuzawa and E. Sweet, "Epigenetics and the Embodiment of Race: Developmental Origins of US Racial Disparities in Cardiovascular Health," *American Journal of Human Biology* 21, no. 1 (2009): 2-15; S.J. Elder, A.H. Lichtenstein, A.G. Pittas, S.B. Roberts, P.J. Fuss, A.S. Greenberg, M.A. McCrory, T.J. Bouchard, E. Saltzman, M.C. Neale, "Genetic and Environmental Influences on Factors Associated with Cardiovascular Disease and the Metabolic Syndrome," *Journal of Lipid Research* 50, no. 9 (2009): 1917-1926; American Anthropological Association, "American Anthropological Association Statement on 'Race,'" www.americananthro.org/ConnectWith AAA/Content.aspx?ItemNumber=2583; and National Research Council, "The National Academies Collection: Reports Funded by National Institutes of Health," in *Critical Perspectives on Racial and Ethnic Differences in Health in Late Life*, ed. N.B. Anderson, R.A. Bulatao, and B. Cohen (Washington, DC: National Academies Press, 2004); Kanjilal, Gregg, Cheng, Zhang, Nelson, Mensah, Beckles, "Socioeconomic Status and Trends," 2348-2355; and Thomas A. LaVeist and John M. Wallace, "Health Risk and Inequitable Distribution of Liquor Stores in African-American Neighborhood," *Social Science & Medicine* 51, no. 4 (2000): 613-617.
[31] Catherine E. Ross and John Mirowsky, "Neighborhood Disadvantage, Disorder, and Health," *Journal of Health and Social Behavior* 42, no. 3 (2001): 258-276; Brian M. Curtis and James H. O'Keefe, Jr., "Autonomic Tone as a Cardiovascular Risk Factor: The Dangers of Chronic Fight or Flight," *Mayo Clinic Proceedings* 77, no. 1 (2002): 45-54.
[32] Michael J. Duncan, Neil D. Clarke, Samantha L. Birch, Jason Tallis, Joanne Hankey, Elizabeth Bryant, Emma L.J. Eyre, "The Effect of Green Exercise on Blood Pressure, Heart Rate and Mood State in Primary School Children," *International Journal of Environmental Research and Public Health* 11, no. 4 (2014): 3678-3688; Eugenia C. South, Michelle C. Kondo, Rose A. Cheney, Charles C. Branas, "Neighborhood Blight, Stress, and Health: A Walking Trial of Urban Greening and Ambulatory Heart Rate," *American Journal of Public Health* 105, no. 5 (2015): 909-913.
[33] Ross and Mirowsky, "Neighborhood Disadvantage, Disorder, and Health," 258-276.

rate, and eventually CVD.[34] Neighborhood disorder included such objective measures as graffiti, vandalism, noise, crime, and abandoned buildings. Even when individual-level socioeconomic status (SES) and socio-demographics were controlled for, including, age, sex, race, education, household income, employment status, occupational status, marital status, and number of children, researchers found that both disadvantage and disorder were associated with poor self-reported health. Walking or outdoor physical activity was not a significant factor, discrediting sole reliance on the health-behavior model. Given their findings, the investigators state: "The daily stress associated with living in a neighborhood where danger, trouble, crime and incivility are common apparently damages health."[35] They concluded by calling for "a bio-demography of stress that links chronic exposure to threatening conditions faced by disadvantaged individuals in disadvantaged neighborhoods with physiological responses that may impair health."[36]

Augustin and fellow researchers sought to measure the bio-demography of stress using a Neighborhood Psychosocial Hazards scale.[37] This scale captured social disorganization by measuring the percent of single parent families, percent of adults without a high school degree or equivalent, and percent of adults divorced, separated or widowed. Public safety was assessed by the number of 911 calls per person per year and violent crimes occurring in the neighborhood. Indicators of physical disorder included percent of vacant houses, number of complaints about street conditions, and number of liquor stores or off-site liquor licenses. Surveying 1,140 randomly selected residents from 65 contiguous neighborhoods in Baltimore with regard to self-reported CVD, they found that those living in the neighborhoods in the highest quartile of psychosocial hazards had four times higher odds of a history of myocardial infarction and more than three times higher odds of other CVD conditions compared to those living in neighborhoods in the lowest quartile, independent of individual-level measures such as age, gender, housing, residential history, smoking history, and education. Thus, the Neighborhood Psychosocial Hazards scale was a better predictor of CVD outcomes than neighborhood-level SES alone.

---

[34] Curtis and O'Keefe, "Autonomic Tone as a Cardiovascular Risk Factor," 45-54; Bruce S. McEwen, "Allostasis and Allostatic Load: Implications for Neuropsychopharmacology," *Neuropsychopharmacology* 22, no. 2 (2000): 108-124.
[35] Ross and Mirowsky, "Neighborhood Disadvantage, Disorder, and Health," 258.
[36] Ross and Mirowsky, "Neighborhood Disadvantage, Disorder, and Health," 258.
[37] Toms Augustin, Thomas A. Glass, Bryan D. James, Brian S. Schwartz, "Neighborhood Psychosocial Hazards and Cardiovascular Disease: The Baltimore Memory Study," *American Journal of Public Health* 98, no. 9 (2008): 1664-1670.

In a third study, using an area probability sample of 639 African Americans living in four different segregated Baltimore neighborhoods with differing socioeconomic and physical characteristics, Mitchell et al. created a neighborhood psychosocial hazards scale comprising the percent of the population living at or below the federal poverty level, the percent of abandoned buildings in the neighborhood, and the violent crime rate per neighborhood.[38] The scale predicted blood pressure, heart rate, history of cardiovascular disease, and smoking behavior. Interestingly, body mass index and waist circumference were not significantly correlated with the psychosocial hazards scale, ruling out obesity (resulting from behavior or genetics) as a cause for the differences.[39]

Thus, the psychosocial stress model predicts health disparities for people living in neighborhoods of concentrated poverty. While certainly genetics, SES, and health behaviors contribute to differential health outcomes, studies suggest that psychosocial stress concomitant with residential segregation holds greater causal and explanatory power. If so, efforts to address, reduce, and perhaps eliminate health disparities should focus less on individual patients or the delivery of particular health care services, and more on initiatives that address concentrated poverty and transform low-income neighborhoods.

BENEFITS TO U.S. HEALTH SYSTEMS FROM RESIDENTIAL SEGREGATION

Given the foregoing, an important question to explore is: how does Catholic health care interface with residential segregation? While care for residents of impoverished neighborhoods is often framed as charity or community benefit, data suggests that the relationship is more mutual or bi-directional. The crux of the matter lies in the current realities of health care reimbursement and financing.

Current reimbursement mechanisms rely on volume. The more frequently a provider sees a patient or groups of patients, the greater the revenue. Like retailers, health care services are generally billed on a per unit basis: "The basic elements of a revenue budget are simple—price and volume. The revenue budget consists of the price charged

---

[38] Cory D. Mitchell, Shari R. Waldstein, Jessica Kelly-Moore, Michele K. Evans, and Alan B. Zonderman, "Neighborhood Socioeconomic Status Is Associated with Cardiovascular Disease Risk Factors in an African-American Cohort," *Annals of Behavioral Medicine* 33 (2007): S31.
[39] Mitchell, Waldstein, Kelly-More, Evans and Zonderman, "Neighborhood Socioeconomic Status," S31.

for each service provided by the unit, department, or organization multiplied by the number of units of service provided."[40] Health care policy has historically attempted to rein in prices by using prospective payment systems such as Diagnosis Related Groups, which predetermine prices for diagnostic categories. But overall, the actionable levers for health systems using traditional reimbursement mechanisms are price and volume, rendering volume, therefore, as one primary factor in a system's financial success.

Consider again our earlier example of CVD. CVD encompasses a cluster of conditions including: high blood pressure, high cholesterol, obesity, and diabetes. Managing these conditions requires frequent medical visits. In fact, patients with chronic conditions such as hypertension and CVD utilize health care services almost three times more than those with optimal cardiovascular profiles. Consequently, people with poor CVD profiles spend almost $6,000 per year more than healthy people.[41] Given its incidence, the total direct and indirect costs for CVD and cerebral vascular conditions in the United States for 2017 was estimated to be a staggering $316 billion.[42] This figure includes health expenditures (direct costs, which include physicians and other professionals, hospital services, prescribed medications, home health care, and other medical durables) and lost productivity resulting from mortality (indirect costs). CVD, as a cluster of conditions requiring high volume treatment, is also highly revenue generating.

What percentage of this spending might we estimate is spent in segregated neighborhoods? Direct calculations have not been published, but initial estimates can be generated statistically. The American Heart Association reports that almost half the adult African-American population (~46 percent) lives with CVD, which equates to approximately 11 million African Americans.[43] Insofar as 50-60 percent of African Americans live in segregated neighborhoods, CVD afflicts roughly 6.5 million residentially-segregated African Americans. This

---

[40] Steven A. Finkler, Cheryl B. Jones, and Christine T. Kovner, *Financial Management for Nurse Managers and Executives*, Fourth Edition (St. Louis: Elsevier Saunders, 2013), 251.
[41] Javier Valero-Elizondo, Joseph A. Salami, Oluseye Ogunmoroti, Chukwuemeka U. Osondu, Ehimen C. Aneni, Rehan Malik, Erica S. Spatz, Jamal S. Rana, Salim S. Virani, Ron Blankstein, Michael J. Blaha, Emir Veledar, and Khurram Nasir, "Favorable Cardiovascular Risk Profile Is Associated with Lower Healthcare Costs and Resource Utilization: The 2012 Medical Expenditure Panel Survey," *Circulation: Cardiovascular Quality and Outcomes* 9, no. 2 (2016): 143-153.
[42] American Heart Association, "Heart Disease and Stroke Statistics 2017 At-a-Glance", www.healthmetrics.heart.org/wp-content/uploads/2017/06/Heart-Disease-and-Stroke-Statistics-2017-ucm_491265.pdf.
[43] American Heart Association, "Statistical Fact Sheet 2013 Update: African-Americans and Cardiovascular Disease," www.heart.org/-/media/data-import/downloadables/african-american-stat-fact-sheet-ucm_319568.pdf. See also American Heart Association, "Heart Disease and Stroke Statistics 2017 At-a-Glance."

suggests that residents of segregated communities may be generating roughly $22 billion in direct and indirect costs annually solely for CVD. Given, however, that CVD incidence is higher in segregated communities, the figure may well be greater.

Thus, though only two percent of the overall United States population, these patients are bearing roughly seven percent of the costs of CVD and thus pay into the United States health system at a disproportionate rate. While this may seem counter-intuitive, a recent study attempted to put cost estimates on this spending disparity. Released in 2012, the National Urban League Policy Institute totaled the costs of United States health disparities at approximately $82.2 billion.[44] Of this, African Americans shouldered $54.9 billion of the total burden—or 67 percent. This comprised $45.3 billion in direct medical costs and $9.6 billion in lost productivity. Many assume that these costs are primarily borne by taxpayers through Medicaid or Medicare. This assumption is wrong, as the study notes:

> Private insurance plans paid 38.4 percent of the healthcare costs associated with disparities ($23 billion). Individuals and families, through out-of-pocket payments, paid 27.7 percent of those costs ($16.6 billion)—more than Medicare and Medicaid combined.[45]

Thus, approximately 66 percent of the $45.3 billion came from out-of-pocket and private insurance sources and was paid for direct health care charges like provider visits. Given that blacks constitute only 13 percent of the total U.S. population and that 26 percent of blacks are poor compared to approximately 12 percent of whites, this figure is even more astonishing. In short, African Americans are shouldering not only an undue burden of health impairments due to residential segregation; they are then financially burdened with an undue portion of health care expenditures for those disparities despite having less income to spend.

Because many health care systems still thrive on volume (rather than value), health systems under current reimbursement strategies not only benefit from adverse effects of residential segregation but may have a vested economic interest in treating the symptoms rather than

---

[44] National Urban League, *"State of Urban Health: Eliminating Health Disparities to Save Lives and Cut Costs,"* nul.iamempowered.com/sites/nul.iamempowered.com/files/tbe_attachments/TBE_2012_50.pdf.
[45] PR Newswire, "Health Disparities Cost U.S. Economy $82b in Higher Healthcare Spending and Lost Productivity," December 5, 2012, www.prnewswire.com/news-releases/health-disparities-cost-us-economy-82b-in-higher-healthcare-spending-and-lost-productivity-182190181.html.

addressing their complex causes.[46] Providers can rest comfortably after prescribing water pills and lifestyle interventions such as diet and exercise, which are only marginally successful for most people over the long-term. So, the more a provider sees Darnell for his diabetes and comorbidities, the more income that provider derives despite the fact that Darnell's condition does not necessarily improve. Providers may argue that this is standard evidence-based care; however, the problem remains. These prescriptions only treat the symptoms rather than the underlying conditions and their causes. In fact, providers have an incentive to maintain the status quo because, if Darnell's health did improve, they would lose much of the revenue he generates. If providers can see people like Darnell frequently while keeping costs as low as possible, the hospital, primary care clinic, or behavioral health practice will thrive even if their patients do not.

Even initiatives to increase access to health care for the underserved can contribute to this problem. Consider the Affordable Care Act (ACA). Recent data suggests that since its launch, the rate of uninsured adults has fallen from a high of 18 percent in Fall 2013 to approximately 12 percent, with approximately 1.8 million blacks being newly covered.[47] If the ACA stays in place, more African Americans will be insured. This will increase access to treatment, but it will also increase health system revenues, while bad or uncollectable debt—a key measure of charity care and community benefit—should decrease.[48] Yet, as before, the underlying causes of the health problems blacks present with their new access to care will remain unaddressed.

What might make a real difference? Compare the results of standard CVD treatment with evidence that moving from a ghetto to a mixed-income neighborhood with few psychosocial hazards can significantly decrease psychological distress, diabetes, and body mass index (BMI).[49] From 1994–1998, the Department of Housing and Urban

---

[46] This is not unique to disparities. U.S. health systems have a vested interest in maximizing reimbursement from the present system and will do so until forced to change. But while this may be equally true for poor black patients and rich white patients, insofar as residential segregation can be categorized as an intrinsic evil, Catholic health systems have an obligation to seek to dismantle this system rather than to profit from or help to maintain it.
[47] Samantha Artiga, Julia Foutz, and Anthony Damico, "Health Coverage by Race and Ethnicity: Changes Under the ACA," *Henry J. Kaiser Family Foundation*, January 26, 2018, www.kff.org/disparities-policy/issue-brief/health-coverage-by-race-and-ethnicity-changes-under-the-aca/.
[48] Michael Wyland, "Redefining Bad Debt and Charity Care," *Nonprofit Quarterly*, March 18, 2016, nonprofitquarterly.org/2016/03/18/redefining-bad-debt-and-charity-care/.
[49] Lisa Sanbonmatsu, Lawrence F. Katz, Jens Ludwig, Lisa A. Gennetian, Greg J. Duncan, Ronald C. Kessler, Emma K. Adam, Thomas McDade, and Stacy T. Lindau, "Moving to Opportunity for Fair Housing Demonstration Program: Final Impacts

Development led a demonstration project called, "Moving to Opportunity" (MTO) in which 4,498 single mothers with children were randomized into three groups: a treatment group of families that received vouchers to move into low-poverty neighborhoods, another group given traditional Housing Choice Vouchers (Section 8), and a control group. The women who moved into low-poverty neighborhoods experienced significantly lower body mass index and glucose levels compared to the traditional voucher and control groups, as well as better mental health.[50] Notably, these physical and mental health improvements occurred despite relatively no change in economic self-sufficiency or individual-level SES.[51]

The MTO study showed that systemic environmental interventions are effective at reducing or eliminating health disparities, but incentive schemes in current reimbursement systems work against organized efforts to engage in such interventions. Let us be clear, we are not saying that all blacks need to be moved from segregated neighborhoods. We are, however, saying that a highly effective solution to health disparities requires intervening at the problem's cause: redeveloping neighborhoods of concentrated poverty into safe, affordable, aesthetically pleasing mixed-income communities, regardless of racial demographics. We do not need to move residents; we simply need to "move" neighborhoods in directions that address underlying causes of health disparities.

These realities, however, present a morally hazardous situation for Catholic health care ministries. The biblical mandate to care for the poor calls Catholic health systems not only to treat the symptom, which is health disparities across race and class lines, but to reduce their fundamental causes. Yet reducing health care disparities for non-integrated urban hospitals would mean a decline in patient revenues. Volume constitutes a significant operational aspect for all health systems, even those engaged in value-based reimbursement schemes. Therefore, most health systems have a vested interest in maintaining the status quo, which may be one reason health disparities have not significantly improved in modern American history despite drastic improvements in medication, clinical techniques, and medical technology.

Evaluation. Policy Development and Research" (Washington, DC: U.S. Department of Housing & Urban Development Office of Policy Development and Research, 2011).
[50] Jens Ludwig, Lisa Sanbonmatsu, Lisa Gennetian, Emma Adam, Greg J. Duncan, Lawrence F. Katz, Ronald C. Kessler, Jeffrey R. Kling, Stacy Tessler Lindau, Robert C. Whitaker, and Thomas W. McDade, "Neighborhoods, Obesity, and Diabetes—a Randomized Social Experiment," *New England Journal of Medicine* 365, no. 16 (2011): 1509-1519.
[51] "Moving to Opportunity (MTO) for Fair Housing Demonstration Project," www.nber.org/mtopublic/.

The potential economic benefits that accrue to health care systems from residential segregation raises a question: are United States health systems complicit in residential segregation? More pointedly, given that Catholic health care provides about 15 percent of all United States health care, is Catholic health care appropriating benefits from the intrinsic evil of residential segregation? M. Cathleen Kaveny helps to illuminate this complex question.

APPROPRIATION OF EVIL

Catholic moral theology has long recognized that in the hurly-burly of real life, our actions are always and everywhere deeply intertwined with those of others. At times, such synergies pair partners committed to the good; other times, we willingly aid and abet others such that we become partners in crime. Most often, however, these interactions are morally murky. We tell ourselves that we seek to do the good, but we know that we are enmeshed—perhaps in ways we cannot fully articulate—with those whose actions strike us as morally problematic. Since the 1700s, the principle of cooperation with evil has helped Catholics wrestle with complex scenarios in an agent (the co-operator) who must decide whether to facilitate or contribute in a subordinate way to a morally unacceptable activity of another actor (the principal agent).[52]

The principle of cooperation was long relegated to the dusty arcana of the moral manuals.[53] The 1994 revision of the ERDs breathed new life into this relatively obscure matrix, positioning it as a central tool for analyzing relationships between Catholic health care institutions and other faith-based or secular entities. More recently, it has been invoked in controversies around the ACA and the contraceptive mandate.[54] Across these loci, it is primarily deployed to negotiate areas deemed intrinsically evil: abortion, tubal ligations and contraception, and physician-assisted suicide.

---

[52] M. Cathleen Kaveny, "Appropriation of Evil: Cooperation's Mirror Image," *Theological Studies* 61, no. 2 (2000): 282. For a comprehensive bibliography on and analysis of moral cooperation see M. Therese Lysaught, *Caritas in Communion: Theological Foundations of Catholic Health Care* (St. Louis: Catholic Health Association, 2014), 55-72, 146-155.
[53] For example, in that staple of pre-Vatican II medical ethics, Gerald Kelly, S.J., *Medico-Moral Problems* (St. Louis: The Catholic Health Association, 1958), the principle of cooperation only appears in the final four-page chapter, 332-335, being used to analyze involvement of Catholic nurses and physicians in "Cooperation in Illicit Operations."
[54] Timothy Jost, "Zubik v. Burwell Briefs Explore Potential Compromise (Update)," *Health Affairs Blog*, April 13, 2016, www.healthaffairs.org/do/10.1377/hblog20160413.054470/full/.

To date, Catholic health care ethics has yet to use this principle to analyze Catholic institutional engagement in structural sin.[55] Neither has the field taken up M. Cathleen Kaveny's insightful identification of a new analytical category, what she refers to cooperation's mirror image—the category of the *appropriation* of evil. Kaveny rightly argues that cooperation does not sufficiently map the landscape of moral ambiguity, leaving invisible or confused the many ways in which "the actions of an agent who is trying to be virtuous can intersect with the morally objectionable acts of others."[56] For Kaveny, a new category is needed to address to situations where an agent does not *contribute* to another's act of wrongdoing but "must decide whether to make use of the fruits of another agent's morally objectionable action," to *incorporate* these fruits into one's own actions in order to further one's own ends or projects.[57] She analyzes examples including: researchers using data from Nazi experiments; consumers purchasing clothing produced by child laborers in developing countries; stem cell researchers using fetal material from elective abortions; and a stay-at-home mother utilizing income from her husband's employment in the nuclear arms industry.[58]

Kaveny's move is insightful and important. However, her analysis remains framed by traditional Catholic moral parameters—focusing primarily on decisions about specific acts made by individual agents. Yet her examples hint at something more. The category of appropriation holds a greater potential for engaging questions that are social and structural in scope. In this section, we briefly discuss Kaveny's understanding of appropriation, identifying additional aspects of the concept embedded in and beyond her original account, with an eye toward outlining a matrix for application.

Kaveny admits that she does not develop "a full-blown analytical framework for appropriation problems" but primarily identifies morally salient features of appropriation problems by carefully teasing out the relationship between cooperation and appropriation.[59] As she notes, cooperation and appropriation problems present the same basic and, in fact, parallel structure. Yet, within this structure, key facets are inverted. For example, cooperation problems are largely *prospective*; potential cooperators must decide if they will contribute to actions that have not yet occurred (e.g., the cabby driving the robber to the bank) or that are ongoing (e.g., providing janitorial services in an abortion clinic). Appropriation is largely *retrospective*; potential appropriators

---

[55] Julie Hanlon Rubio offers one of the few analyses applying the principle of moral cooperation to social ethics in "Cooperation with Evil Reconsidered: The Moral Duty of Resistance," *Theological Studies* 78, no. 1 (2017): 96-120.
[56] Kaveny, "Appropriation of Evil," 286.
[57] Kaveny, "Appropriation of Evil," 280.
[58] Kaveny, "Appropriation of Evil," 280.
[59] Kaveny, "Appropriation of Evil," 307.

must decide if they will utilize products of past actions (e.g., Nazi experimentation) or concurrent actions (e.g., sweatshops) into their own lives and actions to forward their own goals. Likewise, the principal agent's identity differs:

> In cooperation cases, the *auxiliary agent* is the morally conscientious decision-maker who must decide what to do in light of his or her prospective actions likely *contribution* to an evil act performed by the principal agent. In appropriation cases, the roles are reversed. Here, it is the *principal agent* who is the morally conscientious decision-maker, who must decide whether to go ahead with an action that *makes use of* the fruits or byproducts of a morally objectionable act by the auxiliary agent.[60]

Over and against these inversions, the similarities highlight the moral dimensions of appropriation problems. One similarity is what we might call *incorporation*. For example, issues of cooperation do not arise simply by interacting with a wrongdoer (e.g., by sitting on the bus next to one doing something impermissible). Rather, cooperation arises only when one's action might contribute to a wrongdoer's nefarious purposes. Somehow, my action (and, in fact, my person) becomes incorporated into her action, furthering her evil end. Likewise, appropriation only arises when an intended or secondary byproduct of another's morally impermissible action contributes to my own project. In this case, I incorporate the byproduct—and by extension, potentially the act itself—into my own action; it becomes of a piece with my action as it furthers my own substantial ends.

Secondly, for both, *intention* is a crucial though not determinative pivot. In cases of *formal* cooperation—which are always illicit—cooperators "intend, either as an end in itself or as a means to some other end, the wrongdoing designed by the principal agent."[61] The cooperator assents to the wrongdoing and gladly bends her will toward a bad end. Likewise, an appropriator may approve of the wrongdoing that generated the byproduct—a white supremacist might applaud Nazi experiments or a stem cell researcher may support elective abortions. Kaveny refers to this as *ratification*:

> In the appropriation context, ratification of evil is the equivalent of formal cooperation with evil. For an agent to ratify the action of another involves not only taking up its fruits or byproducts and weaving them into his or her own plans and objectives, for that happens in every appropriation case. It also involves stepping into the shoes of the auxiliary agent in a more fundamental manner. When an appropriator ratifies an appropriated action, he or she takes it up and makes

---

[60] Kaveny, "Appropriation of Evil," 287, emphases in original.
[61] Kaveny, "Appropriation of Evil," 284.

Equally Strange Fruit 53

use of it under the intentional description it was given by the auxiliary agent. In effect, the action of the auxiliary agent becomes the appropriator's by adoption. In addition, the appropriator may use that action for the same purposes that the auxiliary agent would have used it.[62]

But what if appropriators do not approve of the actions that generate the by-product? Are they absolved from moral culpability? Here, Kaveny draws parallels with material cooperation. In cases of *material cooperation*, the cooperator does *not intend* the principal agent's morally objectionable actions—her will bends in a different direction. But depending on additional factors, the action may be illicit depending on questions of mediacy and remoteness, namely, "to what degree and in what respect the action of the cooperator overlaps with and contributes to the illicit action of the principal agent."[63] All appropriation entails a material component; might some material appropriation be justified while other less so or illicit?

Parsing these questions requires a more nuanced understanding of intention. Intention, per Kaveny, involves not only assent or agreement with wrongdoers' actions or purposes (ratification); it also requires a dimension of control. Critical to the analysis is whether the appropriator has "any way of influencing decisions about whether or not [the impermissible action] is performed." [64] As she notes, "Intention is purposeful causality; agents cannot intend outcomes over which they know they will have absolutely no influence. Provided that they have nothing to do with its planning or execution, [appropriators do not] intend the wrongful activity that becomes the basis for their own virtuous actions."[65]

Thus, Kaveny distinguishes between intention, wish, and prediction. Wishes and predictions do not cause outcomes. One might *wish* to harm another out of anger, but, if one has no ability to act on it, it cannot be an intention. Likewise, we may be able to make predictions about others' morally impermissible actions.[66] We can *predict* that a certain number of abortions will be performed in the US each year. Some may "build their action plans on the basis of predictions regarding the illicit actions of other people," but, since they have no causal control over these actions, one cannot properly say they intend them.[67]

As with material cooperation, absolving appropriators of intentionality does not necessarily justify their engagement. Even those engaged in remote, mediate material cooperation must do so only for a substantially (or proportionally) grave reason; a substantial good must

---

[62] Kaveny, "Appropriation of Evil," 306-307.
[63] Kaveny, "Appropriation of Evil," 285.
[64] Kaveny, "Appropriation of Evil," 296.
[65] Kaveny, "Appropriation of Evil," 296.
[66] Kaveny, "Appropriation of Evil," 299.
[67] Kaveny, "Appropriation of Evil," 299.

be at stake. This is not primarily because cooperation trades on a utilitarian balancing of goods versus harms. Rather, as Kaveny carefully outlines, it functions within a Thomistic virtue framework. At issue is not solely the harms or evils produced in the world per the action; rather, a primary concern is how the action affects the cooperator's character. Cooperators must be seeking to preserve or promote a substantial good because only by aiming at that good can the ill effect on their character/will caused by the cooperation be mitigated or offset.

Likewise, for Kaveny, appropriation shapes the appropriator's character and, in fact, poses an equal—if not broader—range of moral danger than cooperation. It remains "virtually invisible":[68]

> The main effect of a decision to appropriate the evil action of another is internal; by choosing to tie their action to the evil act of another, appropriators shape their characters in a way that may not have immediate, tangible consequences in the external world. In short, the immediate impact of the decision to appropriate the illicit act of another is a deeply interior one; it alters the character of the appropriator.[69]

> According to [the Catholic moral tradition], the most significant aspect of a human action is the way in which it shapes the character of the person who performs it. Thus, according to traditional Catholic doctrine, individuals who engage in deliberate evildoing harm themselves far more than they do those who suffer injustice at their hands.[70]

How might appropriation impact character? Kaveny names two potential moral dangers: *seepage* and *self-deception*. Seepage refers to the potential for regular involvement with a wrongdoing to desensitize us or subtly shift our moral assessment. As she notes, "If another agent's evil acts contribute in some way to our own objectives, particularly in an ongoing manner, it is difficult not to view them in a more positive light than we otherwise would."[71] Agents who repeatedly engage in a particular action—even the rare but perhaps justifiable taking of human life—"can accustom their hearts and minds to causing the death of another human being....They can easily become desensitized to the sanctity of life, making it easier for them to choose acts that are deliberately disrespectful of other persons in the future." [72]

Likewise, seepage is the slow process of desensitization that leads to self-deception. Self-deception can work on both sides of the action: "In general, whenever an appropriator takes up an auxiliary agent's illicit action or its immediate consequences and makes use of them in

---

[68] Kaveny, "Appropriation of Evil," 289.
[69] Kaveny, "Appropriation of Evil," 289.
[70] Kaveny, "Appropriation of Evil," 303.
[71] Kaveny, "Appropriation of Evil," 307.
[72] Kaveny, "Appropriation of Evil," 304.

a constructive way, the appropriator fuels the auxiliary agent's capacity to discount the wrongfulness of his or her action by pointing to the good that came from it."[73] Equally, appropriators might begin to deceive themselves. Might those who appropriate Nazi data or fetal tissue move beyond seepage and risk "the danger that their own descriptions of themselves as doing nothing more than 'bringing good out of evil'?"[74]

Implicit in Kaveny's account are three additional moral dangers. A first we might call *moral inhibition*. If we come to depend on a byproduct of a morally impermissible action or "accustom ourselves to the benefits that flow from appropriation," might we decide not to take steps "to eliminate the wrongdoing, if the opportunity presented itself,"[75] or might it "mute [our] opposition to the practice or hamper [our] effectiveness in opposing it should the occasion to do so arise"?[76] Here we begin to shade back into intentionality, through sins of omission. Do we find ourselves engaged in what we might call *implicit ratification* by contributing to the sustaining of the activity? Finally, analogous to *scandal*, might appropriation encourage others to more positively assess the morally impermissible act.[77] As she notes, unlike the Nazi experiments that ended fifty years ago, elective abortion remains an ongoing practice in the US. The fact that fetal remains can be put to a worthy scientific use may make others assess the practice of abortion in a morally more positive light.

The category of appropriation, then, provides us with a lens for analyzing those instances where a Catholic agent takes up the fruits or byproducts of other's morally problematic actions. The concepts of incorporation, ratification, seepage, self-deception, moral inhibition, scandal, and implicit ratification provide a matrix for assessing such actions' moral valences. How might this matrix illuminate our question of the relationship between Catholic health care institutions and the economic benefits of residential segregation? What is more, how might Catholic health care's engagement with the social and structural issue of residential segregation deepen the nuances and scope of the category of appropriation?

APPROPRIATION AND RESIDENTIAL SEGREGATION

Catholic health ministries gain revenue for services provided to patients whose health conditions largely result from residential segregation, accruing a benefit from a morally problematic reality. The cate-

---

[73] Kaveny, "Appropriation of Evil," 309.
[74] Kaveny, "Appropriation of Evil," 309.
[75] Kaveny, "Appropriation of Evil," 307.
[76] Kaveny, "Appropriation of Evil," 311.
[77] Kaveny, "Appropriation of Evil," 93.

gory of appropriation of evil illuminates moral contours of this engagement. Simultaneously, this issue helps further develop the framework of appropriation by applying notions of incorporation and intention, specified as ratification, seepage, and self-deception, to considerations of social-structural sin and making more explicit the three additional concepts of moral inhibition, an analog to scandal, and implicit ratification.

We begin with ratification. In potentially benefitting from residential segregation, do Catholic health systems ratify the auxiliary agent's (in this case, society's) wrongful action or structure? Do they "take it up and make use of it under the intentional description it was given by the auxiliary agent," effectively making the action of residential segregation their own by adoption, using it for the same purposes as society (i.e. economic exploitation)?[78] Although at one time Catholic hospitals under Jim Crow endorsed residential and other forms of segregation (by, for example, having separate hospitals for blacks and whites or Whites Only and Coloreds Only waiting rooms, drinking fountains, or other structures), today, at least in their formal rhetoric and mission and value statements, no Catholic hospital or health system explicitly affirms the evil of residential segregation.[79] Certainly, formal ratification is not an issue.

What about the material level? As noted earlier, intention involves not only assent or agreement with wrongdoers' actions or purposes but also a dimension of control or influence over the evil action or outcomes. Do health care organizations have any direct or indirect influence over the realities of concentrated poverty in local neighborhood environments around their facilities? Health care organizations alone cannot eliminate *de facto* residential segregation, but they do have some influence over conditions of local neighborhoods. Historically, Catholic health care located its work and facilities in the poorest communities. Yet, over the past three decades, as Catholic hospitals have merged into health systems, many Catholic hospitals in poor, urban centers have been closed. In fact, hospitals serving poor communities are more likely to close.[80] From 1985-2015, over 300 United States hospitals closed, ten hospitals in urban areas closing per year from 2010-2015.[81] At the same time, health systems—including Catholic

---

[78] Kaveny, "Appropriation of Evil," 307.
[79] Minda, "Catholic Providers Pledge to Address Race, Class-Based Inequity in Health Care." See also Wall, *American Catholic Hospitals*, 74; Andrew S. Moore, "Catholicism and the Civil Rights Movement," *Encyclopedia of Alabama*, www.encyclopediaofalabama.org/article/h-1086.
[80] Melanie Evans, "When a Hospital Closes, Can a Community's Health Improve?" *Modern Health Care*, May 5, 2015, www.modernhealthcare.com/article/20150505/NEWS/150509963.
[81] N. Garg, G. Husk, T. Nguyen, A. Onyile, S. Echezona, G. Kuperman, and J.S. Shapiro, "Hospital Closure and Insights into Patient Dispersion: The Closure of Saint

systems—have followed the strategy of simultaneously or subsequently opening new hospitals in more affluent areas.[82] These decisions, of course, "have been associated with worsened healthcare for the community, especially for the most vulnerable populations."[83] They also have a significant economic impact on poor communities. Many hospitals serve as an area's major employer; closing a hospital negatively impacts a community's employment profile. Research demonstrates the most effective industry at moving people from poverty to middle-income is health care.[84] Ironically, this type of local, community-based workforce development strategy could have the effect of increasing health system revenues because private insurance plans reimburse at higher rates than Medicaid and Medicare.[85] Consequently, by following the trend of closing urban hospitals, Catholic health care has, in fact, often exacerbated realities associated with residential segregation.

Secondly, Catholic hospitals have influence over poor communities through community benefit dollars. In 2011, not-for-profit health care organizations claimed an estimated $24.6 billion in tax exemptions and reported roughly $62 billion in community benefit spending.[86] The most recent study, from 2007, tallied Catholic health care's aggregate community benefit contribution at $5.7 billion.[87] However, despite the community benefit nomenclature, most spending goes to charity care, staff education, mission trips, and well-intentioned but

---

Vincent's Catholic Medical Center in New York City," *Applied Clinical Informatics* 6, no. 1 (2015): 185–199.

[82] Phil Galewitz, "Why Urban Hospitals are Leaving for Fancy Suburbs," *Kaiser Health News*, April 14, 2015, www.governing.com/topics/health-human-services/why-urban-hospitals-are-leaving-cities-for-fancy-suburbs.html.

[83] Galewitz, "Why Urban Hospitals are Leaving for Fancy Suburbs."

[84] Marla Nelson and Laura Wolf-Powers, "Chains and Ladders: Exploring the Opportunities for Workforce Development and Poverty Reduction in the Hospital Sector," *Economic Development Quarterly* 24, no. 1 (2010): 33-44. For a shining example of one Catholic hospital that has prioritized hiring from the local community—St. Bernard's Hospital and Health Care Center in Englewood, Chicago—see Robert J. Gordon, "Inviting the Neighborhood into the Hospital: Diversifying our Health Care Organizations," in *Catholic Bioethics and Social Justice*, ed., M. Therese Lysaught and Michael McCarthy (Collegeville: Liturgical Press, 2018).

[85] Susan J. Penner, *Economics and Financial Management for Nurses and Nurse Leaders*, Second Edition (New York: Springer Publishing Company, LLC, 2013).

[86] Sara Rosenbaum, David A. Kindig, Jie Bao, Maureen K. Byrnes, Colin O Laughlin, "The Value of the Nonprofit Hospital Tax Exemption Was $24.6 Billion in 2011," *Health Affairs* 34, no. 7 (2015): 1225-1233. See also National Health Care for the Homeless Council, "Hospital Community Benefit Funds: Resources for the HCH Community," May 2016, www.nhchc.org/wp-content/uploads/2016/06/policy-brief-hospital-community-benefit.pdf; Bradley Herring, Darrell Gaskin, Hossein Zare, and Gerard Anderson, "Comparing the Value of Nonprofit Hospitals' Tax Exemption to Their Community Benefits," *Inquiry: The Journal of Health Care Organization, Provision, and Financing* 55 (2018): doi.org/10.1177/0046958017751970.

[87] Pamela Schaeffer, "Assessing and Evaluating Community Benefit," *Health Progress* 95, no. 6 (2014): 54-63.

ineffective programs like farmers' markets.[88] In fact, a 2009 national study of non-profit health systems concluded:

> Tax-exempt hospitals spent approximately 7.5 percent of their operating expenses on community benefits. Approximately 85 percent of these expenditures were devoted to charity care and other patient-care services. Of the remaining community benefit expenditures, approximately 5 percent were devoted to community health improvements that hospitals undertook directly. The rest went to education for health professions, research, and contributions to community groups.[89]

Thus, Catholic health care organizations certainly have the resources to influence and address the concentrated poverty associated with residential segregation as a foundational *cause* of health disparities. Certainly, charity care or addressing other individual social determinants of health like individual-level poverty reduction, education, are worthwhile endeavors. However, if physical and subsequently economic structures do not support healthy and safe neighborhoods, these laudable efforts will be counteracted by powerful trends correlated to area of residence.

Thirdly, an even more pressing question must be asked: do Catholic health care organizations—in their staffing, geography, and ethos—reflect and reinforce residential segregation? Structures and financial profiles of health care institutions have changed radically since the Sisters founded Catholic health care in the nineteenth century—even more so since the 1970s. No longer do most health care associates live in the communities they serve. Corporate headquarters are often located in different states. CEOs make multi-million-dollar salaries with bonuses and other incentives. Do organizational decision-makers and the demographics of hospital staffing reflect the population(s) the institution serves? Or do they, in their daily lives, "step into the shoes" of those who affirm residential segregation by where they live? Are local communities given a real voice in institutional decision-making? In short, at issue is the question of intention. If an organization is just as segregated as society, it is hard to argue that the intention of the organization somehow differs from those who engage in and concretize residential segregation.

Thus, while Catholic health care systems might not actively and formally intend the intrinsic evil of residential segregation, they may

---

[88] Farmers' markets increase access to fresh fruits and vegetables, but they can serve to obscure the fact that people need affordable, reliable, and clean grocery stores (just like the suburbs) more than they need farmers' markets. They need structural change that creates jobs and well-being *in* their communities.

[89] Gary J. Young, Chia-Hung Chou, Jeffrey A. Lexander, Shoou-Yih Daniel Lee, and Eli Raver, "Provision of Community Benefits by Tax-Exempt U.S. Hospitals," *New England Journal of Medicine* 368, no. 16 (2013): 1519.

exacerbate it by closing hospitals in poor communities, failing to deploy community benefit dollars to address causes of health disparities, and staffing in ways that reflect and embody societal segregation. Such actions might be called *implicit ratification* parallel to the notion of implicit formal cooperation developed elsewhere.[90] This possibility of *implicit ratification* requires sound multilevel organizational discernment in order to navigate the moral minefield of structural sin.

The concept of appropriation also pushes us to ask questions about other ways that appropriating the benefits of residential segregation might undermine the moral character and well-being of our institutions and associates via seepage, self-deception, moral inhibition and scandal. Seepage: does the fact that health systems benefit financially from residential segregation desensitize associates to the extraordinary dehumanization that these environments inflict? Most people use proxies such as quality of schools and crime rates to search for new neighborhoods in which to reside. By using these proxies, we seek to avoid health-harming neighborhoods. If a neighborhood in its current condition is not fit for health care associates to reside then it probably is not fit for *any* human being without substantial investments. However, our avoidance of these communities often blinds us to the real conditions in which *other* people must live. This willful blindness desensitizes us to the ongoing realities of concentrated poverties and slowly leads to self-deception.

Self-deception: does our 'charitable work' allow us to deceive ourselves, that via free clinics or unreimbursed Medicaid write-offs we are "bringing good out of evil"? Does it allow ourselves to get into habits of seeing ourselves as (largely) white saviors who make a great sacrifice for " these people" who do not even show up for their appointments or take their medications or engage in other actions about which health care associates can devolve into criticism or apathy?[91] Do we allow others—agents of societal racism—to deceive themselves about the evil of these neighborhoods by saying that the Catholic hospitals are there to care for the poor as one of a thousand points of light, so that society does not need to attend to structural determinants?

Moral inhibition: Does our work in these neighborhoods or the way that we conceive health care as occurring only in hospitals or in clinics lead us to see ourselves as unable to do anything to eliminate the evil

---

[90] Thomas R. Kopfensteiner and James F. Keenan, "The Principle of Cooperation," *Health Progress* 76 (1995): 23-27.
[91] See David Hilfiker, *Not All of Us Are Saints: A Doctor's Journey with the Poor* (New York: Hill and Wang, 1994), for a powerful description of how even those dedicated to caring for the poor can become callous, jaded, or agents who participate in blaming the poor for their own oppression.

of residential segregation, seeing the problem as too big or outside the focus of a health care institution?

Scandal: Might our focus on charity care, especially by focusing at the individual patient level, confirm the social biases of many that health disparities are rooted in individual health behaviors or lack of "personal responsibility" among the poor? Alternatively, might it allow others to believe that the ill effects of racial segregation are being taken care of, allowing them to absolve themselves from taking action?

At the root of our attempts to address the illicit appropriation of evil, we must be vigilant for the myriad ways we can devalue others and the ways in which it impacts our character and identity, as individuals and institutions. It is not sufficient to confine our moral discernment to individual level issues; as important as these issues are, as a ministry of the Church, we are called to struggle against dignity-denying principalities and powers (Ephesians 6:12). We are called to be leaven and light of love in dark corners of a world that hungers for the Bread of Life. The Lord asks: "Whom shall I send? And who will go for us?" (Isaiah 6:8). Will Catholic health care respond as Isaiah did? "Here am I. Send Me!" (Isaiah 6:8).

CONCLUSION

We hope this analysis catalyzes conversation in two directions. It appreciates Kaveny's category of appropriation and seeks to develop it by exploring how it might be expanded to institutions, used to examine not only individual actions but structural issues, and to identify other dimensions of appropriation relevant to moral discernment. We call Catholic health care ethicists to take up these three challenges. In addition, we wish to affirm Sister Carol Keehan in pushing Catholic health care toward love and justice by stating, "When anyone is marginalized, because of their race or their ability to pay or their geographic location, all of us have an interest in *repairing the systemic problems at work*."[92] Equipped with new knowledge about relationships between residential segregation and health disparities, no longer is charity alone sufficient (necessary, yes; sufficient, no). Rather, sound community benefit strategies can allow health care institutions to do a sort of penance for the sins of society and their own participation therein. By reimagining and reorganizing community benefit dollars toward community building, Catholic health ministries can serve as witnesses and leaders, coordinating and cooperating with other local health care providers in initiatives that move neighborhoods of concentrated poverty toward health and wholeness; this is healing as

---

[92] Carol Keehan, "Ending Healthcare Disparities: An Urgent Priority and a Growing Possibility," *Frontiers of Health Services Management* 30, no. 3 (2014): 32. Emphasis added.

Christ healed. These benefits accrue not only to the targeted community, but to all communities as crime is reduced, more affordable housing is developed, more jobs are created, incarceration rates are reduced, cities become more livable and sustainable, and health care costs for providers *and* patients are reduced or stabilized.

To their credit, although community health improvement efforts still comprise only roughly 5 percent of community benefit spending (with community building being a smaller percentage of that), Catholic health systems have begun to take steps in this direction. In the ACA environment, the need for charity care and the problem of bad debt has begun to decline. Systems are feeling increased pressure to justify their tax-exempt status.[93] Consequently, some Catholic institutions are starting to engage in community change projects. For example, Dignity Health is working to make some of its communities safer by creating collective efficacy by utilizing mothers and volunteers to keep children safe as they walk to and from school. The system even went so far as to negotiate "with local gangs to keep children secure during the Safe Passage time window."[94] Catholic Health Initiatives has also targeted violence in the communities it serves.[95] Providence focused on Hispanic social isolation in Wilmington, California.[96] Ascension Health is redeveloping communities in Baltimore and Toledo to include mixed-use housing, retail space, as well as space available for community use.[97]

Such interventions need to happen on a larger scale and health outcomes should be measured. Catholic health care alone or in partnership could engage neighborhoods of concentrated poverty by working with community leaders to develop community redevelopment plans with organizations like Purpose Built Communities, which transform poor neighborhoods into thriving low-crime mixed-income neighborhoods without gentrification.[98] Moreover, health systems can engage urban designers to work with neighborhoods to redevelop communities using crime prevention through environmental design (CPTED)

---

[93] Beth Kutscher, "Hospitals Broaden Scope of Community-Benefit Work," *Modern Healthcare*, November 21, 2015, www.modernhealthcare.com/ article/20151121/MAGAZINE/311219988.
[94] Kutscher, "Hospitals Broaden Scope of Community-Benefit Work."
[95] Betsy Taylor, "CHI, Robert Wood Johnson Foundation Map Road to Health," *Catholic Health World*, October 15, 2017, www.chausa.org/publications/catholic-health-world/archives/issues/october-15-2017/chi-robert-wood-johnson-foundation-map-road-to-health.
[96] Renee Stovsky, "Providence Enlists Community to Break Down Isolation in LA Neighborhood," *Catholic Health World*, October 15, 2017, www.chausa.org/publications/catholic-health-world/archives/issues/december-1-2017/providence-enlists-community-to-break-down-isolation-in-la-neighborhood.
[97] Kutscher, "Hospitals Broaden Scope of Community-Benefit Work."
[98] See Purpose Built Communities at purposebuiltcommunities.org/.

principles.[99] This approach, along with working with communities to develop collective efficacy (e.g., neighborhood watch), helps to ensure that neighborhoods are not targets of over-aggressive policing, in which excessive and lethal force is often used as the primary strategy for conflict resolution. Also, as collective efficacy increases, fear of crime decreases.[100]

To be sure, residential segregation will continue to exist, but sound community benefit strategies can ameliorate inhumane living conditions and negative health consequences that result from concentrated poverty. Such an approach to population health benefits communities and improves payer mix, and especially as incentives begin to realign, integrated health systems will also benefit by lowering costs of care, enhancing the common good. To be sure, Catholic health care identifies reducing health disparities as an urgent priority. Yet they must discern if they are working to dismantle unjust systems that lead to poor health outcomes for vulnerable populations or if they are helping to maintain unjust systems through tacitly accepting and maintaining the status quo. Where reimbursement systems do not incentivize actions to address social determinants of health, the mission of Catholic health ministry must serve as the guiding motivation.

The Roman Catholic Church sees itself as "the sacrament of the unity of the human race" (*Catechism*, no. 775). Thus, as a ministry of the Church, Catholic health care organizations must always strive to inculcate and actualize this lofty vocation. Otherwise, we are left with St. John's admonishment:

> We know love by this, that he laid down his life for us—and we ought to lay down our lives for one another. How does God's love abide in anyone who has the world's goods and sees a brother or sister in need and yet refuses help? Little children, let us love, not in word or speech, but in truth and action. And by this we will know that we are from the truth and will reassure our hearts before him whenever our hearts condemn us; for God is greater than our hearts, and he knows everything (1 John 3:16-20). M

---

[99] See International CPTED Association at www.cpted.net/.
[100] Marc L. Swatt, Sean P. Varano, Craig D. Uchida, Shellie E. Solomon, "Fear of Crime, Incivilities, and Collective Efficacy in Four Miami Neighborhoods," *Journal of Criminal Justice* 41, no. 1 (2013): 1-11.

Does Hospital and Health System Consolidation Serve the Common Good?

Michael Panicola

A LOT HAS BEEN GOING ON IN U.S. health care as hospitals, physician groups, insurers, retail pharmacies, technology companies, and others have sought to solidify their position or gain a competitive advantage. The primary means chosen to achieve this end, especially among traditional stakeholders, is one of mergers and acquisitions (M&A), which has resulted in considerable consolidation within an industry that historically eschewed the idea in favor of local or regional health care. Hospitals and health systems have been particularly aggressive in this area. From 1998 through 2017, there were over 1,600 hospital and health system mergers. Although many of these have been small-scale transactions, large systems have become increasingly active, with eleven transactions involving sellers with net revenues of $1 billion or more in 2017.[1]

If this seems like a lot of activity, that is because it is. Powerful forces were and continue to be at play. In the decades leading up to this wave of mergers and acquisitions, the hospitals, physicians, insurers, pharmaceutical manufacturers, and retail pharmacies that make up the U.S. health system were all pretty content with their situation. Sure, there was some maneuvering to further one's edge on the competition, but, for the most part, everyone was reasonably satisfied. Then America started to take notice of the high cost of health care and the questionable value returned on the nation's substantial investment. President Bill Clinton began working in earnest on a reform plan shortly after taking office in 1993, the Republican-controlled Congress passed a spending bill that called for $115 billion in savings through restructuring Medicare in 1997, and managed care became a household term and the primary means of controlling health care costs. Consequently, the once-assumed comfortable profit margins of hospitals began shrinking.

In response, hospital consolidation began accelerating, with freestanding hospitals joining health systems and smaller systems merging

---

[1] Kaufman, Hall & Associates, "2017 in Review: The Year M&A Shook the Healthcare Landscape," www.kaufmanhall.com/resources/research/2017-review-year-ma-shook-healthcare-landscape.

with larger ones. Additionally, these burgeoning health systems started acquiring physician practices in mass (today hospitals employ 42 percent of U.S. physicians). The thinking was that whoever controls the providers and owns the sites of care had the upper hand. Thus, M&A became the winning strategy for hospitals and health systems throughout the 1990s and into the new millennium, with an even greater uptick in mergers since the passage of the Affordable Care Act (ACA) in 2010. In fact, there have been 780 hospital and health system mergers since the start of 2010, including 115 transactions in 2017, which is the highest annual number in recent history.[2]

While this level of M&A activity among hospitals and health systems may benefit a lot of constituents (financial advisors, health care executives, bondholders and investors), something that isn't being asked with enough frequency is whether this is good for U.S. health care and in the best interests of patients and communities. This is a moral question focused on the common good and one that management, boards, and sponsors within Catholic health care, which makes up approximately 20 percent of the U.S. health care system, should be asking. Of interest to this special issue in the *Journal of Moral Theology*, it is also the kind of question that mission leaders and ethicists should be considering versus focusing almost single-mindedly on a narrow set of moral issues that revolve around cooperation. After all, from a moral perspective, the primary motivation for hospital and health system consolidation, should not simply be to obtain a strategic or financial edge over the competition. Rather, because health care is a basic good essential to living a fully human life, the overarching goal should be to make health care better and more accessible and affordable for all. This is the moral lens through which hospital and health system M&A should be viewed generally and particularly for Catholic health ministries, whose ultimate mission is to transform the health of communities, especially those that are physically, economically and socially marginalized, so all persons have an opportunity to flourish and experience God's healing love.[3]

---

[2] Kaufman, Hall & Associates, "2017 in Review."
[3] The notion that health care is a basic good is firmly established in the Catholic social tradition. For instance, in his encyclical *Pacem in Terris*, Pope John XXIII listed health care among those basic human rights that are grounded in the sacredness of life and the inherent dignity every individual possesses (no. 11). Similarly, the United States Catholic Conference of Bishops stated in *Health and Health Care: A Pastoral Letter of the American Catholic Bishops*, no. 18: "This right [to adequate health care] flows from the sanctity of human life and the dignity that belongs to all human persons, who are made in the image of God. It implies that access to that health care which is necessary and suitable for the proper development and maintenance of life must be provided for all people, regardless of economic, social or legal status."

IN-MARKET MERGERS

The majority of hospital and health system mergers, until relatively recently, involved entities within the same or adjacent markets with largely the same patient populations ("in-market" mergers). The presumed benefits often touted by the merging entities are that combined they will operate more efficiently by reducing redundancy and provide better quality care at lower costs. However, a substantial and growing body of evidence suggests otherwise. With the increased market share that accrues through in-market mergers, the combined entities enhance their negotiating leverage with payers and drive up prices, which ultimately get passed on to consumers and make health care less accessible and affordable. The price increases can be quite significant, often exceeding 20 percent when hospitals merge in concentrated markets.[4] Even more concerning is the fact that the diminished competition within markets can negatively impact quality of care, with some studies showing higher mortality rates for patients with certain conditions in highly concentrated markets.[5]

The same negative impact on cost and quality can occur with in-market mergers among physician organizations, especially when they become part of a hospital system and bill payers as hospital outpatient departments.[6] Not only do such mergers tend to be "associated with higher physician prices across a range of services, including three types of commonly billed office visits, office visits across ten prominent specialties… and common outpatient procedures"[7] but also patient outcomes, along some indicators, tend to be worse. A recent study examining the effects of cardiology market concentration on outcomes for Medicare beneficiaries found that "an increase in consolidation leads to statistically and economically significant increases in negative health outcomes." As an example, the authors point out that "moving from a zip code at the 25th percentile of cardiology market concentration to one at the 75th percentile would be associated with 5 to 7 percent increases in risk-adjusted mortality."[8]

---

[4] Martin Gaynor and Robert Town, "The Impact of Hospital Consolidation – Update," *Robert Wood Johnson Foundation Synthesis Report*, www.rwjf.org/content/dam/farm/reports/issue_briefs/2012/rwjf73261.
[5] See, for instance José J. Escarce, Jain K. Arvin, and Jeanette Rogowski, "Hospital Competition, Managed Care, and Mortality after Hospitalization for Medical Conditions: Evidence from Three States," *Medical Care Research and Review* 63, no. 6 (2006): 112S-140S.
[6] Laurence Baker, M. Kate Bundorf, and Daniel Kessler, "Vertical Integration: Hospital Ownership of Physician Practices is Associated with Higher Prices and Spending," *Health Affairs* 35, no. 5 (2014): 756-763.
[7] Brent Fulton, "Health Care Market Concentration Trends in the United States: Evidence and Policy Responses." *Health Affairs* 36, no. 9 (2017): 1530-1538.
[8] Thomas Koch, Brett Wendling, and Nathan Wilson, "Physician Market Structure, Patient Outcomes, and Spending: An Examination of Medicare Beneficiaries," *Health Services Research* 53, no. 5 (2018): 3549-3568.

The Federal Trade Commission (FTC), which is tasked with evaluating the market effects of mergers, has become more critical of the consolidation occurring in health care. In the past several years, the FTC has blocked a number of proposed mergers, including: Boise, Idaho-based St. Luke's Health System's acquisition of the state's largest independent, multi-specialty physician practice group, Saltzer Medical Group; the planned merger of Chicago, Illinois, area health systems, NorthShore University Health System and Advocate Health Care; and the proposed transaction between Hershey, Pennsylvania, based Penn State Health and Harrisburg, Pennsylvania, based PinnacleHealth.

Despite this increased scrutiny on the part of the FTC, anticompetitive market effects caused by the rash of mergers within health care over the last three decades may be too widespread to contain at this point. A recent *Health Affairs* study examining health care market concentration trends in Metropolitan Statistical Areas (MSAs) across the United States, of which there are 382 representing 278 million people, found that in 2016:

- 90 percent of MSAs were highly concentrated for hospitals (up 5 percent from 2010)
- 65 percent of MSAs were highly concentrated for specialist physicians (up 5 percent from 2010)
- 57 percent of MSAs were highly concentrated for insurers (down by less than 1 percent from 2010)
- 39 percent of MSAs were highly concentrated for primary care physicians (up nearly 29 percent from 2010).

Moreover, the author notes that 91 percent of the "382 MSAs analyzed (in which 202 million people resided in 2016) may have warranted either a high or moderate level of concern and scrutiny for at least one of the four products or product groupings."[9]

Of note, concerning levels of concentration within the MSAs were least among health insurers. This would have been quite different had the Department of Justice not successfully sued in 2016 to block the proposed mergers of insurance giants Aetna, Inc., and Humana, Inc., and Anthem, Inc., and Cigna. Perhaps this is why the DOJ argued in its suit that the mergers would "harm seniors, working families and individuals, employers and other health care providers by limiting

---

[9] Brent D. Fulton, "Health Care Market Concentration Trends in the United States: Evidence and Policy Responses," *Health Affairs* 36, no. 9 (2017): 1530-1538.

price competition, reducing benefits, decreasing incentives to provide innovative wellness programs and lowering the quality of care."[10]

Interestingly, of the four groups studied, health insurer market concentration has the most promise of bringing down health care prices. More often than not, however, insurers leverage their enhanced position in the market by raising premiums for employers and individuals, and the price reductions they procure from providers are not passed on to consumers.[11]

One has to wonder to what extent this level of market concentration prevents us from slowing the growth of health spending in the U.S. and how much it contributes to us lagging behind other nations on access and quality metrics.[12] Further research would need to be conducted to know for sure. However, it seems reasonable to conclude that the quasi-monopolizing nature of U.S. health care promotes excessive price inflation and thwarts operational efficiency and clinical innovation.

CROSS-MARKET MERGERS

Whatever the case may be, there is no time to sit idly as we contemplate such matters. More hospital and health system mergers are on the horizon and the most prominent are not of the small scale, in-market variety that result in deep concentration among hospitals or physician organizations. Rather, they involve large health systems with distinct patient populations and no overlapping markets ("cross-market" mergers). Three recent examples include: (1) the Englewood, Colorado, based Catholic Health Initiatives (CHI) merger with San Francisco, California, based Dignity Health, which would create one of the nation's largest nonprofit health systems with over $28 billion in net revenues and care sites spanning twenty-eight states; (2) the now green-lighted merger among Aurora Health Care and Advocate Health Care, both the largest health systems in their respective states of Wisconsin and Illinois, which will lead to a system with $11 billion in net revenues; and (3) the recently announced merger between Cincinnati, Ohio, based Mercy Health and Marriottsville, Maryland, based Bon

---

[10] Office of Public Affairs, "Justice Department and State Attorneys General Sue to Block Anthem's Acquisition of Cigna, Aetna's Acquisition of Humana," *United States Department of Justice*, July 21, 2016, www.justice.gov/opa/pr/justice-department-and-state-attorneys-general-sue-block-anthem-s-acquisition-cigna-aetna-s.

[11] See, for instance, Brent D. Fulton, "Health Care Market Concentration Trends in the United States: Evidence and Policy Responses," *Health Affairs* 36, no. 9 (2017): 1530-1538, and Richard Scheffler and Daniel Arnold, "Insurer Market Power Lowers Prices in Numerous Concentrated Provider Markets," *Health Affairs* 36, no. 9 (2017): 1530-1538.

[12] Eric Schneider, Dana Sarnak, David Squires, Arnav Shah, and Michelle Doty, "Mirror, Mirror 2017: International Comparison Reflects Flaws and Opportunities for Better U.S. Health Care," *The Commonwealth Fund*, July 2017, interactives.commonwealthfund.org/2017/july/mirror-mirror/.

Secours Health System, which combined would establish a health system with $8 billion in net revenues with hospitals and other care sites across seven states.

What should we expect from these types of cross-market mergers? Will they enhance the pricing power of the combined entities and result in steep increases in the cost of health care services, as we have seen with in-market mergers? Or will they deliver on the promises being touted by the leaders of these organizations? CHI and Dignity claim that combining the organizations "will create a stronger system to increase investment in critical areas to advance quality of care and access. The new organization will have the size and ability to scale best-in-class clinical service lines; recruit and retain top talent; standardize operations to improve quality and reduce the cost of care; advocate more effectively for all people, especially those who are poor and vulnerable."[13] Similarly, the leaders of Aurora and Advocate contend that the "merger is about transforming care delivery and reimagining the possibilities of health as bigger meets better and size meets value to benefit consumers. By joining forces we will be able to expand our network to scale innovation and create a destination in the Midwest for patients and the talented clinicians who care for them."[14] With much more emphasis on improving the health of communities, Mercy Health and Bon Secours note, "This merger strengthens our shared commitment to improve population health, eliminate health disparities, build strength to address social determinants of health, and invest heavily in innovating our approaches to health care."[15]

These statements resemble those of hospitals and health systems that completed in-market mergers in the past. While the evidence surrounding those mergers was not favorable from a cost or quality standpoint, it would be wrong to assume the same holds true for cross-market mergers given the lack of geographical overlap. Each such merger should be assessed on its own merits—some may benefit patients and communities while others may not. What does the evidence tell us? Here we are a bit more limited as the studies of cross-market mergers are not quite as extensive as they are for in-market mergers. Leemore Dafny, the Bruce V. Rauner Professor of Business Administration at the Harvard Business School and a member of the faculty of the Kennedy School of Government, is one of the leading figures conducting research in this area and finds some evidence prices rise even when

---

[13] See "Why are the two organizations combining?" in "FAQs," *Catholic Health Initiatives*, www.advancinghealthcaretogether.org/faqs/.
[14] Aurora Health Care, "Advocate and Aurora to Merge, Creating Top 10 Health System Poised to Transform the Industry," December 4, 2017, www.aurorahealthcare.org/media-center/news-releases/advocate-and-aurora-to-merge-creating-top-10-health-system.
[15] Alex Kacik, "Mercy Health and Bon Secours to Merge," *Modern Healthcare*, February 21, 2018, www.modernhealthcare.com/article/20180221/NEWS/180229982.

merging hospital groups are in different markets in the same state. In 2016, Professor Dafny and colleagues published a detailed study on the topic, within which they concluded:

> We find that hospitals gaining system members in-state (but not in the same geographic market) experience price increases of 6-10 percent relative to control hospitals, while hospitals gaining system members out-of- state exhibit no statistically significant changes in price. The former group is likelier to share common customers and insurers. This effect remains sizeable even when the merging parties are located further than 90 minutes apart. The results suggest that cross-market, within-state hospital mergers appear to increase hospital systems' leverage when bargaining with insurers.[16]

Perhaps further research will corroborate this study and we need not worry about potential negative effects associated with cross-market mergers involving health systems with no overlapping states. If we assume there is little to no leverage gained through these types of mergers, why, then, would health systems that are already quite sizeable and complex want to merge at all?

Bigger Makes Better
One reason, which both CHI-Dignity and Aurora-Advocate specified in their public statements, is that merging will enable the combined entities to operate more efficiently and provide better care at a lower cost. Certainly, this is possible when, among other things: the culture, values, leadership styles, strategic vision and operational priorities of the organizations align; the organizations have deeply embedded processes that systematically drive quality improvement and a business model geared toward making health care more accessible and affordable; and there is effective pre- and post-merger management. However, the evidence does not point in this direction with most mergers.

Integration of large health systems, especially when operational challenges are already present, is terribly difficult. Even some of the simplest financial synergies can be hard to obtain. A 2012 McKinsey & Company study of hospital mergers points out: "Over the past 20 years, hundreds of hospitals around the world have merged, and in many cases, perhaps most, the arrangements did not deliver the desired outcomes."[17] A more recent analysis by PWC states: "The implicit

---

[16] Leemore Dafny, Kate Ho and Robin Lee, "The Price Effects of Cross-Market Mergers," March 18, 2016, www.kellogg.northwestern.edu/docs/faculty/dafny/price-effects-of-cross-market-hospital-mergers.pdf.
[17] Penny Dash, Jonathan Dimson, David Meredith, and Paul White, "Marry in Haste, Repent at Leisure: When Do Hospital Mergers Make Strategic Sense?" *McKinsey &*

logic of these arrangements is that by getting larger, hospitals and healthcare systems will generate scale and reduce operating costs while still delivering the same level of care—or better. Yet, based on our experience, most transactions have failed to deliver the promised benefits of scale."[18]

Given the questionable results of many mergers, it is fair to challenge the assumption that bigger is better and to ask why health systems with billions of dollars in annual revenue need to get even larger to be more efficient and innovative. Some health systems are decidedly moving away from this strategy. For-profit Franklin, Tennessee, based Community Health Systems, Dallas, Texas, based Tenet Healthcare, and Brentwood, Tennessee, based Quorum Health are but three examples of systems selling hospitals and other struggling assets that have dragged down financial performance.

Moreover, the largest for-profit hospital chain, Nashville, Tennessee, based HCA Healthcare, is being very selective with its hospital acquisitions, though it recently announced it has signed a letter of intent to acquire Mission Health, a six-hospital nonprofit health system based in Asheville, North Carolina. HCA's broader strategy, however, is to expand its reach in outpatient care, especially ambulatory surgery centers where growth opportunities exist. Toward this end, HCA was rumored to be partnering with a private equity firm to acquire Nashville, Tennessee, based Envision Healthcare, whereby HCA would have assumed control of Envision's 255 surgery centers across the U.S. had it won the bid.[19] Though unsuccessful as Envision was sold for $5.6 billion to private equity firm KKR, HCA will continue to be active in the outpatient services space through acquisitions and organic growth.

Nonprofit health systems might want to take notice of this trend to downsize hospitals and direct capital to outpatient services, especially since they were the acquirers in nearly 75 percent of hospital acquisitions in 2017, and their strategies tend to lag behind those of for-profit systems. Some nonprofit health systems, such as St. Louis, Missouri, based Ascension Health, one of the largest nonprofit health systems in the U.S. with nearly $23 billion in net revenues, have already started to move in this direction. Ascension recently signaled its intent to shift

---

Company, www.mckinsey.com/~/media/McKinsey%20Offices/United%20Kingdom/PDFs/When_hospital_mergers_make_strategic_sense_.ashx.
[18] Anil Kaul, K.R. Prabh, and Suman Katragadda, "Size Should Matter: Five Ways to Help Healthcare Systems Realize the Benefits of Scale," *PwC*, March 15, 2016, www.strategyand.pwc.com/reports/size-should-matter.
[19] Jeff Byers, "HCA, KKR Reportedly Make Bid for Envision Amid Deal Frenzy," *Healthcare Dive*, May 21, 2018, healthcaredive.com/news/hca-kkr-envision-possible-buyout/523949/.

its strategic focus from hospitals to outpatient access points and telemedicine services.[20] Ascension has also suspended merger talks with similarly-sized Renton, Washington, based Providence St. Joseph Health, which itself has made significant strides in innovating its business model and care delivery system to better meet the needs of consumers, patients, and communities.

Buying Security

A second reason often cited in favor of large scale, cross-market mergers is that they can enhance the financial security of the combined entities, with the bigger system being better able to withstand market vicissitudes, reimbursement reductions, and changing patterns of consumer behavior. Indeed, Jim Skogsbergh, CEO of Advocate Health Care, seemed to have this in mind when he commented recently, "Coming together will allow us to be better prepared to weather the storms."[21]

There may be some merit to this claim, as increased assets can provide a nice cushion for rainy days and generate additional non-operating income to be used to support operations and fund capital projects when operating income trends downward. The additional assets and financial heft can also enable larger health systems to build infrastructure for and experiment more freely with value-based care initiatives without the same degree of trepidation smaller systems may have around failing. Still, though, this only holds true if the combined entities perform reasonably well. Poor financial performance does not discriminate among larger and smaller health systems. While larger systems may be able to withstand down periods longer, the increased size does not inoculate them from the deleterious effects of operational inefficiency and financial underperformance. Merging should not hinge simply on bolstering the balance sheet but on whether it makes sense from a broad strategic perspective that includes, first and foremost, the benefits to patients and communities.

Responding to the Competition

A third reason health systems are eagerly embracing large scale, cross-market mergers is that their traditional business model and revenue stream is being upset by alternative payment models, changes in consumer behavior, and a wave of disruptive competitors. Coming off

---

[20] Alex Kacik, "As Ascension Restructures, It Hints at Smaller Hospital Footprint," *Modern Healthcare,* March 22, 2018, www.modernhealthcare.com/article/20180322/NEWS/180329953/ascension-amid-major-restructuring-hinting-at-smaller-hospital.
[21] Reed Abelson, "Hospital Giants Vie for Patients in Effort to Ward Off New Rivals," *New York Times,* December 18, 2017, www.nytimes.com/2017/12/18/health/hospitals-mergers-patients.html.

of some tough years during the Great Recession, health systems benefited significantly from the influx of new consumers brought on by Medicaid expansion and the ACA marketplaces. The boon to business was short-lived, however, and more recently health systems have faced considerable financial pressures despite serving more patients year-over-year. In addition to rising labor and supply costs as well as bad debt due to the proliferation of high-deductible health plans, inpatient volumes are waning as consumers are becoming more cost-conscious and more care is being delivered in lower-cost outpatient settings.

Most health systems have been slow to adapt to the changing landscape, clinging instead to an outdated, capital-intensive acute/specialty care infrastructure that has served them well for many years while driving up the costs of health care to unsustainable levels. Meanwhile, a slew of independent primary care organizations—ChenMed, Iora Health, Oak Street Health, to name a few—are seizing the opportunity engendered by the new market dynamics. The common denominator among these organizations is that they are providing high-quality care in convenient settings at lower costs mainly through meticulous management of patients and attention to patients' social and economic factors that affect health. In so doing, they are taking business away from hospitals by reducing emergency department visits and hospitalizations upwards of 40 percent compared to fee-for-service primary care groups.[22]

The scale of some of these disruptive primary care organizations may not yet be substantial enough to force health systems into a course correction. However, collectively their efforts are having an impact and also being complemented by much larger health care companies that want to cut even deeper into the hospital business, which accounts for over 30 percent of U.S. health care expenditures. Pharmacy chain and benefits manager CVS's announced $69 billion acquisition of Aetna, the third largest health insurer in the U.S. with over $63 billion in net revenues and twenty-three million members, is just one example of this disruption. With its 1,100 in-store Minute Clinics, CVS is poised to become a primary care hub for Aetna members as well as others across communities in thirty-three states.

Another example is the acquisitions made by Optum, a division of UnitedHealth Group, the nation's leading health insurer with over $184 billion in net revenues and seventy million members. In early 2017, Optum acquired Surgical Care Affiliates (SCA) for $2.3 billion, bringing into its fold SCA's 190 owned or operated ambulatory surgery centers and surgical hospitals serving roughly one million pa-

---

[22] See, for instance, Robert Pearl, "Lessons on Disrupting Primary Care," November 13, 2017, robertpearlmd.com/lessons-disrupting-primary-care/.

Hospital and Health System Consolidation 73

tients in over thirty states. Later in 2017, Optum announced it was acquiring DaVita Medical Group for $4.9 billion. Through the acquisition, Optum will add 17,000 physicians, three hundred medical clinics, thirty-five urgent-care locations, and six outpatient surgery centers across six states to its existing base of more than 30,000 medical providers.

Not to be left out, Anthem, the second-largest health insurer in the U.S. with over $89 billion in net revenues and forty million members, has reportedly entered into an agreement to acquire Nashville, Tennessee, based Aspire Health, the nation's leading community-based palliative care provider with contracts established with more than twenty health plans serving consumers in twenty-five states. Through its innovative algorithms identifying patients with complex, serious illness, Aspire mobilizes comprehensive care teams to address patient needs in the home, focusing on symptom management, patient-family communication, advance care planning, and care coordination.

Lastly, news just came out that retail giant Walmart is in early-stage talks to partner with or even acquire Humana, the nation's fourth largest health insurer with over $54 billion in net revenues and fourteen million members. While it may not be possible to predict the outcome of these and similar transactions, it is safe to say that they are part of a larger plan meant to further marginalize hospitals. Beyond these moves, disruption is coming from previously unheard of places. Tech giants like Amazon, Apple, Google, and Microsoft accelerated their efforts in 2017 to redesign health care by investing in health startups and applying their core business strengths to improve people's health.

One example of this is Amazon's move potentially to enter the pharmacy business by applying for and receiving wholesale distribution licenses from twelve state pharmaceutical boards. This threat alone may be what led to the recent announcement that the largest standalone pharmacy benefits manager, Express Scripts, which could see its business cut into by Amazon, was being acquired for $67 billion by Cigna, the nation's fifth leading health insurer with over $54 billion in net revenues and fifteen million members.

Another example of big-tech's push into health care is Apple's recently announced launch of subsidiary AC Wellness, a group of state-of-the-art primary health clinics for its own employees and their families, which opened in the spring of 2018. Apple also recently announced that it is developing an iOS feature that would allow consumers to access their electronic medical records on their phones.

Of course, the buzz early in 2018 was about Amazon, Berkshire Hathaway, and JPMorgan Chase's announcement that they are coming together to form an independent health care company aimed at improving care and reducing costs for their more than 1 million U.S. employees. The first step toward this end was selecting Dr. Atul Gawande as CEO of the new company. Dr. Gawande, who currently practices general and endocrine surgery at Brigham and Women's Hospital and is a professor at the Harvard T.H. Chan School of Public Health and Harvard Medical School, is a bold pick on a number of levels. With Dr. Gawande you get the perfect "insider-outsider," someone who has intimate knowledge of the health system and its many opportunities yet is not steeped in traditional health system thinking and will bring creative ideas to the table in an effort to make health care more accessible, affordable and better for all.

This is a lot for hospitals and health systems to absorb. The ground is changing under them at a furious pace, causing them to rethink their traditional strategies. Large-scale, cross-market mergers have become one strategy health systems are employing to reestablish their footing in the competitive health care environment. Whether this strategy contributes to the betterment of U.S. health care and the long-term sustainability of health systems is questionable. One thing is certain, if cross-market mergers are simply an attempt to reclaim lost monopolistic leverage rather than improve health care access, affordability, and quality, health systems will be doomed to fail because change is proceeding inexorably.

CONCLUSION

Health systems do not have to be the victims or culprits in the current reshaping of U.S. health care. They can be part of the solution, complementing the efforts of disruptive companies that are having a positive impact on the access, cost, and quality problems that have plagued the U.S. for decades. To do this, though, health systems need to disrupt themselves, become more resilient and adaptable, and not wait as forward-thinking competitors build insurmountable leads. Disruption from within will require many things of health systems, including: radically rethinking current structures and management practices that may be encumbering and hinder a system's ability to adapt swiftly to changing community needs, consumer behaviors and competitive threats; shifting from a traditional hospital business model to one focused on providing high-quality care at low costs in convenient settings where services are needed as opposed to areas with the best payer mix; reimagining strategies with an emphasis on value-based care and population health versus maximizing high-margin service lines and expensive, low value procedures; rationalizing hospital assets in response to changing utilization trends and population health needs and, when possible, repurposing facilities to support community need and development; allocating capital differently by directing the majority of available funds toward value-based care modes of delivery rather than acute/specialty care structures and technology; retraining members of the hospital workforce to avoid massive lay-offs and meet the growing needs of outpatient care and telehealth; and engaging in creative public and private cross-sector partnerships to address disparities in health caused by social, economic and environmental inequities.

It will be a major undertaking for health systems to disrupt themselves, and it will not be easy. However, for health systems, the status quo is failing and mergers that are intended to preserve hospital-centrism are not going to prove successful in the end. Sure, there will always be a market for hospital and specialist services, but macro- and micro-economic factors are coalescing in such a way that the good old days will never return. Health systems that double down on hospital-centric strategies, hoping that current trends pass, will become commodities and cost centers for those leading the transformation of U.S. health care.

Speaking at the Federation of American Hospitals convention in Washington DC, in early March 2018, Health and Human Services Secretary Alex Azar made this abundantly clear when he warned hospital executives that the Trump Administration is determined to take steps aimed at improving health care and lowering costs. "Today is an opportunity to let everyone know that we take these shifts seriously, and they're going to happen—one way or another. The administration and this president are not interested in incremental steps. We are unafraid of disrupting existing arrangements simply because they're backed by powerful special interests."[23]

Management, boards, sponsors, and mission/ethics leaders would do well to focus on the disruption that needs to occur within to enable health systems to transition to value so that health care can be more accessible and affordable for all. Moreover, given the suspect nature of in-market mergers and the uncertain benefits of cross-market mergers, they should evaluate M&A opportunities through the moral lens of whether they will help speed this transition to value and ultimately enable health systems to take a leading role in transforming the health of communities, especially those that are physically, socially and economically marginalized. Ⓜ

---

[23] Jessie Hellmann, "Trump's Health Chief Warns Hospital Execs about Health Care Costs," *The Hill*, March 5, 2018, thehill.com/policy/healthcare/376789-trumps-health-chief-warns-hospital-execs-about-health-care-costs-change-is.

Accompaniment with the Sick: An Authentic Christian Vocation that Rejects the Fallacy of Prosperity Theology

Ramon Luzarraga

AN HISTORIC STRENGTH OF THE Christian faith is that its sole central symbol was an instrument designed to inflict maximal human suffering and death. The cross, a tool of execution used by a number of ancient peoples and societies,[1] whose use was perfected by the Roman Empire as a sequence of stages of a procedure of humiliating, torturing, and executing criminals,[2] shows the world a religion with the ability to confront and grapple with human suffering and death. That God was killed on such a punitively violent appliance proclaims to the world a God who understands human suffering and death to its fullest measure. What happened after the cross is God's promise that suffering and death never have the last word. Our problem as Christians has been, and remains, that instead of reminding ourselves of these lessons and confronting suffering and death ourselves, we succumb to the cultural bias of the present day, the human temptations to run away from it or explain it away.

The recurring challenge for Christians is to deal with the human reality of suffering and death without the extremes of either despair against God or romanticizing the reality where its tragic nature gets explained away. On the one hand, we want to encourage people to turn to God and ask for help, trusting that God will not respond with indifference. On the other hand, we do not want to insult the sick and the dying with well-intentioned but vapid statements such as "God will not give you what you cannot handle." The late Father Desmond Crotty, who was pastor of my parish in New Orleans, bluntly described the Cross in a Good Friday homily by shouting to his assembled parishioners: "It hurt!" The reality of suffering and death, like the Cross, hurts physically, mentally, and emotionally. The sick and the dying do stumble and knuckle under the pressure. This same thing happened to Christ carrying His cross. Among his last words on the Cross was his echoing the Twenty-Second Psalm, crying out in lament in Matthew 27:46, "My God, my God, why have you forsaken me?!"

---

[1] Martin Hengel, *Crucifixion* (Philadelphia: Fortress Press, 1977), 22-23.
[2] Hengel, *Crucifixion*, 25-27.

Accompaniment with the Sick 77

The last thing those who are suffering need to hear are pithy statements of positive thinking which afflict them precisely because they fail to acknowledge the reality that should be obvious to those with eyes to see and ears to hear.

A contemporary manifestation of this challenge is the way too many U.S. Christians resolve suffering through prosperity theology. This false idea, presented by too many Christian ministers, is that human suffering is somehow tied wholly to one's own emotional and mental disposition. With enough prayerful entreaties to God and a strong show of faith, this theological perspective claims that God will grant the suffering person the sufficient amount of grace to control, or even overcome, his or her own suffering and pain. Some ministers make the bold claim that one could name the illness, cast it out in Jesus's name like a demon, and recover one's health.[3] The consequences of this false theology are devastating to the Christian. Those who cannot overcome their suffering may be left with a strong, lingering doubt about whether God loves them or even whether God exists. Worse still is how this type of prosperity theology transfers responsibility to the

---

[3] This is not something restricted to the margins of Christianity. I have heard charismatic Catholic priests in their preaching reduce depression to being a bad spirit which can be cast out in Jesus's name. They ignore the complexity of depression, which is something even many Catholic saints suffered. According to the Catholic Bishops of California, "Indeed, men and women of strong moral character and heroic holiness – from Abraham Lincoln and Winston Churchill to St. Thérèse of Lisieux, St Benedict Joseph Labre, St. Francis of Rome and St. Josephine Bakhita – suffered from mental disorders or severe psychological wounds" (Bishops of California, *Hope and Healing: A Pastoral Letter from the Bishops of California on Caring for those who Suffer from Mental Illness Addressed to all Catholics and People of Goodwill* (Sacramento: California Catholic Conference, 2018), 5). But, what about saints who not only embrace, but seek out suffering, following the example of Christ's suffering for the expiation of sin in the world? This is a feature of Catholic devotional literature, which still carries much influence on the faithful, even today. For example, Saint Lydwine of Shiedam, was a young, beautiful woman beset by a succession of health afflictions which, over time, destroyed her beauty, her health, and eventually cost her life. Faced with a strong temptation to despair of God, a pair of skilled spiritual directors counselled her to see her suffering, not as punishment from God for her own sins, but as an offering to God to suffer for the souls of others afflicted by sin as Jesus did. Her spiritual journey got to a point where she wished she could suffer more for others. Saint Lydwine's example is not unique among the saints. But, it brings up a question, should we run to embrace suffering like she did? Ronda Chervin correctly concludes that Christ would not override human free will and allow ever increasing levels of suffering in imitation of Him unless the person consents to a call from Him to do that. Therefore, vocations like that of Saint Lydwine of Shiedam are rare. If a patient feels called to such a vocation, it would require discernment under a skilled spiritual director, so the person afflicted would avoid lapsing into self-pity, despair of God's love and salvation, or perhaps self-glorification where one grandstands over one's holiness in suffering, which is a distortion of the same. See Ronda Chervin, *Avoiding Bitterness in Suffering: How Our Heroes in Faith Found Peace Amid Sorrow* (Manchester: Sophia Institute Press, 2015), 200-202.

person suffering. The sick person carries the entire burden to overcome his or her illness. Pithy statements made by Christians offering support to the sick, in this context, are in fact statements of abdication of the responsibility all Christians have to show compassion and accompany those who suffer.

This article traces out how prosperity theology itself is a corruption of a Calvinist idea describing the meaning and purpose of earthly prosperity, including good health, as a sign of God's blessing. It has been secularized to the point where Americans often think that those who suffer are somehow ultimately, or exclusively, responsible for their situation in life. I then argue how this idea served as a catalyst for the dangerous idea of "positive thinking." This idea implies, and sometimes makes explicit, that those who are suffering somehow deserve their situation and, therefore, must earn healing with faith in God expressed through the correct positive intellectual, emotional, and spiritual disposition.

I conclude with a retrieval of the theology of accompaniment to refresh a Catholic understanding of suffering which can serve as a rebuttal to the negative influence of positive thinking and prosperity theology. This idea of accompaniment is common among Latin American and U.S. Hispanic theologians and has gained greater international exposure through the writings of Pope Francis. Retrieving the idea of accompaniment with the suffering sick serves two purposes. First, it combats the false idea that those who suffer can and should endure a disproportionate burden of handling their illness and suffering by themselves. Alone, the sick must demonstrate an ability to exercise sufficient faith in God to receive the needed strength for surviving illness and, perhaps, claim and receive healing. The theology of accompaniment can counter this error because it can update a long and venerable Christian understanding of human suffering being redemptive because of its participation in the sufferings of Christ. Those who suffer draw strength precisely because they know God in Christ accompanies them in their suffering, because he experienced the worst kinds of human suffering and therefore understands it to the fullest measure. Second, accompaniment theology avoids both human beings' attempt to run away from the reality of suffering by placing distance between themselves and the sick and the romanticization of suffering where people attempt to talk away the existence of the all-too-real physical pain and mental anguish through positive thinking. Instead, accompaniment calls on persons to imitate Christ's accompanying us in our suffering. This is accomplished by us accompanying those who suffer. The reason a Christian does not run away from suffering is because Christ did not. Instead of trying to explain away suffering and pain, Christians unite in solidarity with the suffering sick and with Christ and hope in his promise that illness and suffering never have the last word. This is not a passive hope but the hard work of active resistance to assert life in the face of physical illness and its negative mental and spiritual effects which seek to reduce and extinguish life.

THE CALVINIST ROOTS AND EVOLUTION OF POSITIVE THINKING

Prosperity theology traces its roots to the Calvinist Protestant religious foundations of most of the original thirteen colonies that became the United States. Here, a caution is in order. Although I claim this idea emerged out of a specific strand of Protestant Calvinist theology, it is not representative of the entirety of Protestant theological thought throughout its history. Harvey Cox argues that "the sources for this type of theology are a certain kind of distorted Calvinism. One reading of it says that if you're doing well materially, God must favor you. It's a sign that you are one of the elect. If you're not doing so well, you must not be one of the elect. There's a real motivation to do well in worldly terms—to bring assurance that you were really in the Kingdom of God. That's found its way into American preaching and religion right up through Norman Vincent Peale and *The Power of Positive Thinking*."[4] Though this strand of theology was preoccupied with wealth in its early stages of development, health as a measure of one's faith in God and a measure of God's favor to the person would soon follow.

This evolution began with John Calvin himself, who argued that material goods were not necessarily bad, so long as we followed Scripture's instructions as to their use. "For if we are to live, we have also to use those helps necessary for living. And, we also cannot avoid those things which seem to serve delight more than necessity. Therefore we must hold to a measure so as to use them with a clear conscience, whether for necessity or for delight."[5] While Calvin thought such arguments constituted "a godly counsel" designed to combat "this dangerous evil," it was too severe because they went beyond what Scripture required.[6] Now, Calvin is not naïve. He readily acknowledged that people will "seek an excuse for the intemperance of the flesh in its use of external things [and] pave the road to licentious indulgence."[7] However, he insisted that Christians find the "general rules for lawful use of wealth" in Scripture alone, and not what he saw as the "definite and precise legal formulas" of Patristic theologians and medieval scholastics.[8]

Calvin's theological heirs in the United States once dominated the religious scene to the point that "most of the churches were decidedly

---

[4] Paul Massari, "God and Money," *Harvard Divinity School*, Oct. 4, 2014, hds.harvard.edu/news/2014/10/07/god-and-money#.
[5] John Calvin, *Institutes of the Christian Religion*, ed. John T. McNeill, trans. Ford Lewis Battles (Philadelphia: The Westminster Press, 1960), III, x, i.
[6] Calvin, *Institutes*, III, x, i.
[7] Calvin, *Institutes*, III, x, i.
[8] Calvin, *Institutes*, III, x, i.

Calvinist in their theology" despite the pluralism of their religious practices and differences in the specifics of doctrine.[9] They brought with them Calvin's views concerning wealth and expanded them. Beyond their rejection of the Patristic and medieval suspicion of the individual's acquisition and use of wealth, these Calvinists thought that "a modest gain on one's investment was considered good business sense and commendable in the eyes of God, who expected his stewards to increase their wealth."[10] Of particular influence were the Puritans, who claimed that "God's will argued that men must be diligent in business and that, if they were among the predestined saints, their business ventures would thrive."[11] It is a short step from that Puritan teaching to its consequence: the belief that prosperity served as sign of being among God's elect, an outcome of obedience to living according to God's commands. The lack of prosperity was a sign of divine disfavor or punishment, the responsibility for which rested with the individual.

This Calvinist idea of prosperity as a sign of God's election was filtered through the radical individualization of Christian faith caused by the Second Great Awakening (1800–1830). Church power, influence, and authority in churches got dispersed, and, in its place, the most successful Christian movements thrived on democratic popular appeal.[12] Despite the broad repudiation of Calvinism caused by this particular awakening,[13] that Calvinist, Puritan idea of prosperity as a sign of election survived and continued to develop through the late nineteenth and early twentieth centuries. Kate Bowler describes two important strands of this development: the "Gospel of Wealth" and "positive thinking." With the United States in the throes of the social displacement and prosperity of post-Civil War Gilded Age industrialization, alongside the Social Gospel movement led by ministers like Walter Rauschenbusch and the Salvation Army, founded by William and Catherine Booth, there emerged ministers like the Baptist Russell H. Conwell who preached a Gospel of Wealth. This updated the received Calvinist, Puritan idea of prosperity as a sign of God's favor by arguing that one is called by God to work hard and see God's hand in the emerging industrial, capitalist economic order. In that order, pov-

---

[9] William G. McLoughlin, *Revivals, Awakenings, and Reform* (Chicago: The University of Chicago Press, 1978), 38.
[10] McLoughlin, *Revivals, Awakenings, and Reform*, 28.
[11] McLoughlin, *Revivals, Awakenings, and Reform*, 27.
[12] Nathan O. Hatch, *The Democratization of American Christianity* (New Haven: Yale University Press, 1989), 65.
[13] See McLoughlin, *Revivals, Awakenings, and Reform*, 114–129.

erty was equated with sin, and wealth was the product of dutiful virtue.[14] The storm and stress of modern business was a test for the Christian to become more hard-working, innovative, pragmatic, open to risk, and self-reliant.[15]

In this rapidly evolving and disorienting American social and economic milieu, many Christians lacked confidence in their own ability to fulfill God's will through the virtues celebrated by the Gospel of Wealth. They sought a new way to "close the gap between earnest faith and divine blessings" through divine assistance. This is where the idea of "positive thinking" first gained currency. Positive thinking argued that those with "right thinking" would be rewarded with material prosperity and health.[16] However, there were two conditions. The first was to align one's self to God through faith. God was portrayed as a provider who promised abundance, understood as material prosperity, to believers.[17] Several ministers called for, even demanded of their congregations, a demonstration of this faith through tithing to their respective ministries.[18] The second condition was to hold a belief that to align oneself with Jesus Christ in faith can yield better health if one willfully sought his healing power, or declared oneself cured in his name. Because human beings are created in God's image, a person's brain possessed sufficient power to control one's whole body[19] in order to receive and channel this healing power. Jim Bakker, a once-prominent prosperity Gospel preacher, was representative of this claim of positive thinking when he wrote "the organs of your body can heal or die by their mental attitude."[20] He and other preachers went so far as to claim that a good "confession" of faith where one named one's need, be it health, wealth, or another thing, was enough to secure a blessing from God to fulfill that need. If one's need was not fulfilled, that was understood to be a sign of a lack of faith in God.[21]

In sum, "prosperity theology claims a power rooted in the operation of faith. Believers conceptualize faith as a causal agent, a power that actualizes events and objects in the real world. Faith acts as a force that reaches through the boundaries of materiality and into the spiritual realm, as if plucking objects from there and drawing them back into

---

[14] Kate Bowler, *Blessed: A History of the American Prosperity Gospel* (New York: Oxford University Press, 2013), 31-32.
[15] Bowler, *Blessed*, 32.
[16] Bowler, *Blessed*, 31.
[17] Bowler, *Blessed*, 34.
[18] Bowler, *Blessed*, 98-100.
[19] Bowler, *Blessed*, 142-143.
[20] John Wigger, *PTL: The Rise and Fall of Jim and Tammy Faye Bakker's Evangelical Empire* (New York: Oxford University Press, 2017), 67.
[21] Wigger, *PTL*, 66.

space and time."[22] Positive thinking thrived with the economic prosperity during and after World War One, adapted during and survived after the Great Depression, and thrived anew with the renewed economic prosperity of the Second World War and post-war era.[23] At that time, positive thinking disappeared as a uniquely Christian phenomenon because it was incorporated into the cultural mainstream of the United States.[24]

Here, the widespread damage by "positive thinking" to the physical and spiritual health and well-being of persons, reveals itself. First, the prosperity theology and its supporting ideas are grounded in a gross misinterpretation of Scripture. Harvey Cox points out that biblical texts which speak of abundance and prosperity have "the message that God doesn't want you to be poor and starving. That's a message for poor people. God doesn't will you to be poor. He doesn't want you to be starving. He wants you to have what you need to live."[25] Preachers who interpret such passages as God wanting wealth and health as we understand it today imply that such levels of the same existed in the time and situation the Bible was written. To the contrary, in a pre-modern economy where the bulk of wealth was held in land holdings, agricultural production, or livestock, wealth could easily be lost in a political or environmental crisis. A critical reading of the Book of Job yields a powerful illustration of this fact. Prosperity theology reads into the Bible levels of physical and economic well-being unimaginable even to the pharaohs of Egypt, the kings of Babylon, or the emperors of Rome.

On the backs of this foundationally faulty understanding of Scripture is the inevitable crisis triggered when requests for health and wealth are not granted by God despite the most fervent prayers and acts of faith. Bowler identifies four ways believers would interpret why they have not been healed of their illness. These include a suspension of judgment where one would not draw any conclusions about the reason why another remained ill, a belief that the believer has failed to win the "spiritual battle against illness," that the illness may be a sign of righteous suffering along the lines of Job, or a questioning of their church's teaching on faith healing, which may lead to the loss of faith in their church or, worse, their loss of faith in God.[26]

However, the mainstreaming of positive thinking does not limit the crisis to Christians alone. The failure to prosper, including being healed of disease, has been secularized to the point that most Americans believe that somehow poverty and illness are to be blamed on the

---

[22] Bowler, *Blessed,* 141.
[23] Bowler, *Blessed,* 37-39.
[24] Bowler, *Blessed,* 36.
[25] Massari, "God and Money."
[26] Bowler, *Blessed,* 175-177.

Accompaniment with the Sick 83

person suffering. The social commentator Barbara Ehrenreich quotes Jimmie Holland, a psychiatrist at Memorial Sloane Kettering Cancer Center, who wrote: "It began to be clear to me about ten years ago that society was placing another undue and inappropriate burden on patients that seemed to come out of the popular beliefs about the mind-body connection. I would find patients coming in with stories of being told by well-meaning friends, 'I've read all about this—if you got cancer, you must have wanted it....' Even more distressing was the person who said, 'I know I have to be positive all the time and that is the only way to cope with cancer—but it's so hard to do. I know that if I get sad, or scared, or upset, I am making my tumor grow faster and I will have shortened my life.'"[27]

Ehrenreich concludes by stating, "the failure to think positively can weigh on a cancer patient like a second disease."[28] The sick are called to suppress those "understandable feelings of anger and fear, all of which must be buried under a cosmetic layer of cheer."[29] Therefore, despite the fact that the Gospels show Christ himself crying out in pain and anguish on the cross, the sick are allowed to shed nary a tear, lest they enable their illness. Friends and family of the sick try to rationalize why they contracted the disease in the first place and transfer their responsibility to accompany the sick in their suffering to medical professionals, who are paid to manage their patients' illness and pain. Meanwhile, the sick are left isolated because their friends and family are unable or unwilling to help them deal with the reality of what is causing their suffering.

A THEOLOGY OF ACCOMPANIMENT AS A REBUTTAL TO PROSPERITY THEOLOGY

The theologically sound solution to the fallacy of prosperity theology and the negative consequences of positive thinking is a theology of accompaniment of those who suffer. Its strength is grounded in the fact that Jesus Christ understands human suffering because he experienced it himself. Kallistos Ware describes this experience of Christ as enabling him to be in tangible direct solidarity with those who suffer. Ware grounds his argument in Hebrews 4:15, a passage he considers to be the most important Christological text in the New Testament. "For we do not have a high priest who is unable to sympathize with our weaknesses, but one who has similarly been tested in every way, yet without sin." Ware interprets that passage to mean that Jesus, when he became incarnate, assumed a human nature that was fallen. "Christ lives out his life on earth under the conditions of the fall. He is not

---

[27] Barbara Ehrenreich, *Bright-Sided: How the Relentless Promotion of Positive Thinking has Undermined America* (New York: Metropolitan Books, 2009), 43.
[28] Ehrenreich, *Bright-Sided,* 43.
[29] Ehrenreich, *Bright-Sided,* 41.

himself a sinful person, but in his solidarity with fallen man he accepts to the full the consequences of Adam's sin. He accepts in full not only the physical consequences, such as weariness, bodily pain, and eventually the separation of the body and soul in death. He accepts also the moral consequences, the loneliness, the alienation, the inward conflict."[30] This description easily encompasses the ugly features of illness: physical, emotional, and spiritual.

Jesus's solidarity with humanity in their suffering is salvific because through his sufferings in life, which climaxed with his torture and execution on the cross, he shows that God actually accompanies us in our suffering. Our suffering is never an abstraction for God, who gets it. Pope Francis builds on this tradition articulated by Ware. Jesus, through his resurrection, promises that suffering and death do not determine human destiny. "The incarnate Son of God did not remove illness and suffering from human experience but by taking them upon himself he transformed them and gave them new meaning. New meaning because they no longer have the last word."[31] Therefore, instead of having us run away from illness and suffering through positive thinking or making transactional claims on his power, Jesus promises to accompany us through suffering and death to a new and resurrected life. Those who suffer illness are not to suffer alone. If Jesus accompanies each of us through illness, suffering, and death then all Christians must imitate him by modeling our behavior to the sick by accompanying them.

What does it look like to accompany the sick in imitation of Christ? While the theology of accompaniment is a regular feature of Pope Francis's writings, including those concerned with the pastoral care of the sick, it was pioneered by Latin American and U.S. Hispanic theologians. The theology of accompaniment was a key pastoral principle the Catholic Church in Latin America employs in its strategy for evangelization and for the training of clergy and lay ministers for that evangelization. In the concluding document of the Fifth General Conference of the Latin American Episcopal Conference, then-Cardinal Jorge Mario Bergoglio wrote that "each sector of the People of God asks to be accompanied and formed, in keeping with the particular vocation and ministry to which it has been called…. Training is therefore required for those who can accompany others spiritually and pastorally."[32] Consequently, each and every Christian vocation must include this feature of accompanying those persons who we serve. As

---

[30] Kallistos Ware, *The Orthodox Way, Revised Edition* (Crestwood: St. Vladimir's Seminary Press, 1995), 75.
[31] Pope Francis, "Message for the Twenty-Second World Day of the Sick 2014," December 6, 2013, w2.vatican.va/content/francesco/en/messages/sick/documents/papa-francesco_20131206_giornata-malato.html.
[32] Conference of Latin American Bishops, *Aparecida Concluding Document*, 282.

pope, Francis repeats the idea of accompaniment as integral to the lived vocation of the Christian in his first apostolic exhortation, *Evangelii Gaudium*. "The Church will have to initiate everyone – priests, religious, and laity – into this 'art of accompaniment' which teaches us to remove our sandals before the sacred ground of the other (cf. Ex. 3:5). The pace of this accompaniment must be steady and reassuring, reflecting our closeness and our compassionate gaze which also heals, liberates, and encourages growth in the Christian life" (no. 169).

In contrast to our society's avoidance, even fear of encountering illness, suffering, or death, which prosperity theology and positive thinking do nothing to contradict, Pope Francis invites Christians to call on the Holy Spirit for the grace to resist the temptation toward avoidance and denial when faced with those who suffer illness. The sick, instead of being abandoned as failures in the practice of faith in God, are accompanied as part of the vocation of being a Christian as articulated by *Aparecida*. Only through the practice of this vocation can the Christian realize the intrinsic, irreducible value of those who suffer illness and the time spent accompanying them through their struggles. Francis writes, "With lively faith let us ask the Holy Spirit to grant us the grace to appreciate the value of our often unspoken willingness to spend time with these sisters and brothers who, thanks to our closeness and affection, feel more loved and comforted. How great a lie, on the other hand, lurks behind certain phrases which so insist on the importance of 'quality of life' that they make people think that lives affected by grave illness are not worth living!"[33]

Pope Francis goes further and describes the daily experience of accompaniment as occasions for giving thanks to God precisely because one has been given a vocation by God. "Those who generously assist the sick, beginning with family members, health workers and volunteers, to give thanks for their God-given vocation of accompanying our infirm brothers and sisters."[34] This is not mere sentimentalist cant on his part. The vocation of accompaniment of the sick is grounded in

> The supreme commandment of *responsible closeness*...as we see clearly from the Gospel story of the Good Samaritan (cf. *Lk* 10:25-37). It could be said that the categorical imperative is to never abandon the sick. The anguish associated with conditions that bring us to the threshold of human mortality, and the difficulty of the decision we have to make, may tempt us to step back from the patient. Yet this is

---

[33] Pope Francis, "Message for the Twenty-Third World Day of the Sick 2015," December 3, 2015, w2.vatican.va/content/francesco/en/messages/sick/documents/papa-francesco_20141203_giornata-malato.html.
[34] Pope Francis, "Message for the Twenty-Fifth World Day of the Sick," December 8, 2016. w2.vatican.va/content/francesco/en/messages/sick/documents/papa-francesco_20161208_giornata-malato.html.

where, more than anything else, we are called to show love and closeness, recognizing the limit that we all share and showing our solidarity.[35]

In direct contradiction to both prosperity theology and positive thinking, Pope Francis argues that, for a theology of accompaniment to be authentic, its practitioners cannot run away from the reality of human suffering or illness. Pope Francis points to Jesus and Mary as exemplars of accompaniment. He writes that,

> Faith in God is on the one hand tested [by sickness], yet at the same time can reveal all of its positive resources. Not because faith makes illness, pain, or the questions which they raise disappear, but because it offers a key by which we can discover the deepest meaning of what we are experiencing; a key that helps us to see how illness can be the way to draw nearer to Jesus who walks at our side, weighed down by the Cross. And this key is given to us by Mary, our Mother, who has known this way at first hand.[36]

In other words, the test of faith is to accompany the suffering sick as Mary accompanied the suffering Jesus on his way to being crucified. Faith in God is shown in part by accompanying those weighed down by the cross of illness. What Pope Francis said to a prayer gathering with prisoners in a Philadelphia jail reveals that we are called to do nothing less than "to share your situation and to make it my own... [to] pray together and offer our God everything that causes us pain, but also everything that gives us hope, so that we may receive from him the power of the resurrection."[37]

Roberto Goizueta, in his systematic theology of accompaniment, articulates the fruits of what Pope Francis speaks to. Accompaniment with the sick transforms a situation of despair into one of hope. "It is the corporate, shared character of suffering, undertaken in mutual solidarity, that distinguishes suffering from mere debilitating sadness and makes possible our common struggle against suffering."[38] Goizueta points out the error of positive thinking. Illness and suffering when

---

[35] Pope Francis, "Message to the Participants in the European Regional Meeting of the World Medical Association," November 7, 2017, w2.vatican.va/content/francesco/en/messages/pont-messages/2017/documents/papa-francesco_20171107_messaggio-monspaglia.html.
[36] Pope Francis, "Message for the Twenty-Fourth World Day of the Sick 2016," September 15, 2015, w2.vatican.va/content/francesco/en/messages/sick/documents/papa-francesco_20150915_giornata-malato.html.
[37] Francis, "Visit to Detainees at Curran – Fromhold Correctional Facility," in *The Words of Pope Francis: From Cuba to Philadelphia A Mission of Love* (Vatican City: Libreria Editrice Vaticana, 2015), 415.
[38] Roberto S. Goizueta, *Caminemos con Jesús: Toward a Hispanic/Latino Theology of Accompaniment* (Maryknoll: Orbis Press, 1995), 183.

borne alone debilitates because an individual's strength is sapped by illness. However, accompaniment does not mean that "misery likes company." Instead, by accompanying one in suffering, it is more bearable for the person who is ill because more are carrying that burden. What follows is resistance to the suffering by sharing a life together, which reasserts life in the face of illness. This is why Goizueta argues "that solidarity in the midst of suffering is what reveals to us the ultimate powerlessness of suffering: our common life, manifested in our relationships of solidarity, overcomes all attempts to destroy that life. Suffering shared is suffering already in retreat."[39] This includes those who are suffering chronic illness and those who face death.

This idea of Goizueta's does not romanticize or deny the physical and mental anguish of suffering in any way. To the contrary, solidarity engenders a resistance to suffering and illness in the hope that in Jesus Christ, through his death and resurrection, life has the last word. Goizueta's confidence is rooted in the very idea with which we began: Jesus experienced it himself. Jesus went to his death fighting and resisting the temptation to succumb to feeling abandoned by God. This is, ironically, evidenced by his cry out to the Father.[40] His fighting suffering and death is already a rejection of the same, and his resistance is vindicated by the Resurrection. Those who accompany the sick form a similar community of resistance in relationship to each other and God, in the hope, the expectation, that this suffering and death do not have the last word, but, instead, new life with God is our shared destiny.

The prosperity Gospel, with its empty promises of faith eliminating illness and yielding health, holds great sway in U.S. society. Christians who work in any ministry will encounter this among the faithful who suffer illness, especially those who work in Church-sponsored health ministries. When the prosperity Gospel inevitably fails believers and leaves them thinking themselves to be a failure for not having sufficient faith in God to heal themselves, the Christian must be prepared to intervene with a truthful alternative.

All Christians are called not to waste their suffering on wishful thinking. The Christian must find a path of growth where he or she can gain an understanding that illness, pain, and suffering can and do yield human and supernatural benefits.[41] What is needed is a sound theology which tells those who are sick that they should not bear this burden alone. Whether the Christian is a health professional who treats the sick on a daily basis or the majority of us faithful who offer care to suffering family, friends, and neighbors as needed, Jesus offers a

---

[39] Goizueta, *Caminemos con Jesús*, 183.
[40] Goizueta, *Caminemos con Jesús*, 184.
[41] Benedict M. Ashley, O.P. and Kevin O'Rourke, O.P., *Ethics of Human Care*, Third Edition (Washington, DC: Georgetown University Press, 2002), 197.

model of accompaniment. He accompanies us in our suffering illness because Scripture shows that he himself accompanied those who suffered and died. Jesus understands our suffering because he suffered to the point of death. As Mary accompanied Jesus in his suffering, even to the Cross, we Christians accompany each other in our suffering. Jesus and Mary both challenge us to find ways not to waste our suffering through fatuous promises of a prosperity that will never come while communicating a false optimism that seizes on nothing other than the contents of our wallets. Jesus and Mary model accompaniment with those who suffer to open a path for us all to conversion to a hope. This hope is God's promise to us all that a life with God and our neighbor can be lived even in a state of illness. God can be known more truly despite illness and suffering. Even in the face of death, the life God gifted each of us will always have the last word. M

Grace at the End of Life: Rethinking Ordinary and Extraordinary Means in a Global Context

Conor Kelly

IN THE CATHOLIC CONTEXT, health care is a true work of grace. The healing, accompaniment, and caring at the heart of health care all show the imprint of a God whose love is incarnate in the world.[1] One essential task for Catholic health care ethics, then, is to promote a form of ethical discernment that not only allows people to weigh the concrete choices before them but also invites them to be attentive to the unfolding of grace in their lives. While every issue in contemporary health care is potentially open to this kind of twofold analysis, decisions about care at the end of life are especially poignant from this point of view because two simultaneous movements of grace always need to be held in tension. On the one hand, temporal life needs to be recognized and respected as a gift from God. On the other hand, the good of eternal life must be acknowledged as an even greater gift of grace.

Traditionally, Catholic health care ethics has used the principle of ordinary and extraordinary means to navigate this tension, since the distinction ensures that the gift of life is neither dismissed too cavalierly nor esteemed too absolutely. In theory, this approach recognizes and affirms the work of grace in both the fight to preserve life and the willingness to forgo certain treatments, but, in practice, the division has been used to suggest that the true path of grace lies only at one end of the spectrum. This reduction does serious theological damage both speculatively—by preemptively narrowing the space in which one conceives of grace at work in the world—and practically—by restraining ordinary Catholics' abilities to cooperate with grace in their own lives. Furthermore, in an environment of significant global health disparities, this narrowing tendency has the power to exacerbate some of today's worst health-related injustices. Catholic health care ethics must respond to this contemporary trend or else it will fail in its service to the people of God. The purpose of this article, then, is to analyze

---

[1] For a nice explanation of how grace functions in Catholic health care, see Neil Ormerod, "Health Care and the Response of the Triune God," in *Incarnate Grace: Perspectives on the Ministry of Catholic Health Care*, ed. Charles Bouchard (St. Louis: CHA USA, 2017), 22–36.

the developments reinforcing a narrow view of grace at the end of life and to propose solutions that will counteract their force so that Catholic health care ethics might more thoroughly respect the Catholic community's faith in the continual prospects of grace at all stages of life.

In pursuit of this end, the article has three parts. The first part reexamines the well-known distinction between ordinary and extraordinary means, illustrating how both elements of this division originally facilitated a proper respect for life as a gift of grace and then explaining how recent trends have transformed the principle into a tool that restricts the work of grace all but exclusively to the fight to preserve life. Next, the second part of the paper argues that this ballooning of the category of ordinary means cannot be justified in a world of dramatic health care inequities. In response, part two builds on the growing scholarly insistence that Catholic health care ethics needs to be in closer contact with social ethics, arguing specifically that the line between ordinary and extraordinary means needs to be interpreted in a global and not just a local context. The main result of this reconceptualization is to remove the onus of moral obligation from some of the costlier routine procedures whose burden levels seem reasonable in a United States context but truly extraordinary when viewed from a global perspective. Finally, the third, concluding section of the article discusses some of the structural changes that will be necessary to make this new approach to ordinary and extraordinary means a more realistic option for more of the faithful today.[2] Together, the three parts present a challenge to the current approach to end-of-life care while also offering a unique set of resources for the church to employ as it seeks to support and to encourage the faithful to work in good conscience to discern how God is calling them and their family members to respond to the complexities of grace at the end of life.

---

[2] The focus on structural changes stems from the assumption that social structures have the power to exert a causal, but not deterministic, effect on moral agents, variously making certain decisions easier or harder to make. As a result, structural forces must be considered when a new approach to moral discernment is countenanced because the incentives embedded in social structures affect both the likelihood that an agent will entertain a new form of discernment (e.g., discern ordinary and extraordinary means in light of a larger social consciousness) and the likelihood that he or she will act in a way that is consistent with the results of that discernment. See Daniel K. Finn, "What is a Sinful Social Structure?" *Theological Studies* 77, no. 1 (2016): 136–164.

ORDINARY AND EXTRAORDINARY MEANS AND THE WORK OF GRACE

In Catholic health care ethics, the distinction between ordinary and extraordinary means is a fundamental resource for moral discernment. Historically-conscious ethicists note some version of the distinction as early as the sixteenth century, and the patron saint of moral theology, Alphonsus Liguori, advanced the idea explicitly.[3] In its original iterations, the principle of distinguishing ordinary and extraordinary means was not about health care per se but about one's personal moral obligations for self-care more generally.[4] Of course, the means in question were always means of preserving life, but the context for this reflection was not bioethics as it is conceived today but something more like meta-ethics. In particular, these moralists accepted Thomas Aquinas's assertion that "whatever is a means of preserving human life, and of warding off its obstacles, belongs to the natural law" (ST I-II, q. 94, a. 2, c). Their main concern was therefore to determine how far one's natural law obligation to preserve his or her own life might extend. For example, the sixteenth century Dominican Francisco de Vitoria framed the question around "the specific obligation of the human person to eat food and thus sustain life," asserting that one ought to distinguish between the positive obligation to attain nourishment and the permissible, but not obligatory, effort to secure better quality foods as part of that endeavor.[5] Other moralists reflected on similar concerns, and the eventual conclusion of their debates was that a person only had to exhaust his or her energy and resources to procure the ordinary means of sustaining human life, including, in the words of Gerald Kelly's twentieth century review of the earlier tradition, "the use of reasonably available food, drink, medicines and medical care; the wearing of sufficient clothing; the taking of necessary recreation; and so forth."[6] One's natural law obligations did not, however, extend to the extraordinary means of preserving life—that is, "everything which

---

[3] James F. Keenan, S.J., "A 400-Year-Old Logic," *Boston College Magazine*, Spring 2005, bcm.bc.edu/issues/spring_2005/ft_endoflife.html#keenan; in "When Burdens of Feeding Outweigh Benefits," *Hastings Center Report* 16, no. 1 (1986): 30–32, John Paris points to the Dominican Domingo Bañez as the originator of the term in 1583. Alphonsus Liguori quoted in Scott M. Sullivan, "The Development and Nature of the Ordinary/Extraordinary Means Distinction in the Roman Catholic Tradition," *Bioethics* 21, no. 7 (2007): 386–397.
[4] Donald E. Henke, "A History of Ordinary and Extraordinary Means," in *Artificial Nutrition and Hydration and the Permanently Unconscious Patient: The Catholic Debate*, ed. Ronald P. Hamel and James J. Walter (Washington, DC: Georgetown University Press, 2007), 53–77.
[5] Henke, "A History of Ordinary and Extraordinary Means," 55–56.
[6] Gerald Kelly, S.J., "The Duty of Using Artificial Means of Preserving Life," *Theological Studies* 11, no. 2 (1950): 203–220, 204.

involves excessive difficulty by reason of physical pain, repugnance, expense, and so forth."[7]

Notably, these extraordinary means involved a number of medical treatments, so it is not surprising that the larger idea of distinguishing ordinary and extraordinary means of preserving life has become intimately connected with health care ethics today. Indeed, such a development is a logical extension of the tradition, since health care is the primary field in which humans have to adjudicate various means of preserving life. Nevertheless, it is important to remember that the roots of this distinction go beyond health care to larger matters concerning one's general moral obligation. Significantly, this broader focus on moral responsibility, and not just health care decision-making, allows one to see the relationship between the classic distinction and the work of grace more clearly in two ways.

First, the distinction presumes grace in its conclusion that certain means will be obligatory. The reason there is a *duty* to preserve life is that life is a gift from God. This is a direct conclusion from Aquinas's description of this duty as a universally binding precept of the natural law, for he averred as a matter of definition that the "natural law is nothing else than the rational creature's participation of the eternal law" (ST I-II, q. 91, a. 2, c). Insofar as the duty to preserve life was an evident principle of the natural law, it was also in alignment with God's eternal law and therefore an affirmation both of God's role as the author of life and, by extension, the giftedness of life itself.[8] The subsequent specification of this duty through the concept of ordinary means begins with this assumption and underscores it, ensuring a proper appreciation of the magnanimity of life as a gift of grace.

Second, the distinction between ordinary and extraordinary means also creates space for grace in the decision to forgo extraordinary means of preserving life. The major premise behind this distinction was the belief that the preservation of life is a general precept of the natural law. Against this background, the novelty of the distinction is not that humans would need to use ordinary means to preserve life but that some means might actually be extraordinary and for that reason not obligatory. Arriving at this conclusion required some alternative— or at least additional—understanding of grace's operation at the end of life, such that the termination of a gift of grace (i.e., life) might nevertheless serve as its own source of (new) grace. As one might imagine, Christian faith in the resurrection provided the basis for this interpretation, for hope in the afterlife implies, as David Kelly has put

---

[7] Kelly, "The Duty of Using Artificial Means," 204.
[8] William May makes this point rather explicitly in *Catholic Bioethics and the Gift of Human Life,* Second Edition (Huntington: Our Sunday Visitor, 2008), 276.

it, that "the present life is to be treasured, but it is not all there is."[9] Such was the clear conclusion of Pope Pius XII in his influential statement on the "Prolongation of Life," which defended the non-obligatory nature of extraordinary means by arguing that "life, health, all temporal activities are in fact subordinated to spiritual ends."[10] This position takes nothing away from the sanctity of life as a gift of grace; instead, it adds another level of appreciation for the next life as a wonderful gift of grace as well.

For the field of Catholic health care ethics, with its keen interest in the work of grace in the world, these two observations point to one fundamental reality about the traditional distinction between ordinary and extraordinary means: both sides of this distinction serve to call attention to the role of grace amidst serious illness. Consequently, Catholic health care ethics should be rightly concerned when the narrative begins to suggest that grace is primarily—or worse, exclusively—found at only one end of the division. Unfortunately, the popular use of this principle in recent years, at least in the U.S. context, has begun to suggest exactly this idea. The clearest way to see this is in the interpretation and application of Pope John Paul II's 2004 allocution on "Life Sustaining Treatments and Vegetative State."

In that allocution, John Paul II stressed the inherent dignity of the human person, criticizing the trend to dehumanize patients in a "persistent vegetative state" on the basis of their reduced functionalities and instead emphasizing the intrinsic worth of every human life. In order to ensure the protection of life even in this vulnerable state, John Paul II addressed the issue of obligatory care for those in a persistent vegetative state, and professed, "The administration of water and food, even when provided by artificial means, always represents a *natural means* of preserving life, not a *medical act*. Its use, furthermore, should be considered, in principle, *ordinary* and *proportionate*, and as such is morally obligatory."[11] Although the language "in principle" left some room for discernment in specific cases, the force of this allocution was almost immediately evident as moral theologians began to debate how authoritatively and definitively a papal allocution could assign artificial nutrition and hydration to the category of ordinary

---

[9] David Kelly, *Medical Care at the End of Life: A Catholic Perspective* (Washington, DC: Georgetown University Press, 2006), 5.
[10] Pope Pius XII, "The Prolongation of Life," in Ronald P. Hamel and James J. Walter, *Artificial Nutrition and Hydration* (Washington, DC: Georgetown University Press, 2007), 91–97.
[11] Pope John Paul II, "Address to the Participants in the International Congress on 'Life-Sustaining Treatments and Vegetative State: Scientific Advances and Ethical Dilemmas,'" March 20, 2004, w2.vatican.va/content/john-paul-ii/en/speeches/2004/march/documents/hf_jp-ii_spe_20040320_congress-fiamc.html. Emphasis in original.

means.[12] Additionally, the Congregation for the Doctrine of the Faith (CDF) eventually responded to a request for clarification about this allocution, further elevating the significance of the teaching and prompting renewed discussions about this proposal among those actively engaged in health care ministry.[13] The impact of this papal address was especially pronounced in the United States, where it played into the ongoing culture war battle over the fate of Terri Schiavo, a Florida woman in a persistent vegetative state whose Catholic parents were locked in a legal battle with her husband over whether to remove her feeding tube.[14] As that subtext makes clear, the effect of the allocution was to cement the idea that artificial nutrition and hydration ought to be identified *prima facie* as an ordinary means of preserving life, despite the fact that a compelling case can be made for the interpretation that this is precisely not what the allocution meant in practical terms.[15] Whatever the authoritative status of the allocution and its interpretation, the *prima facie* reading certainly had a lot of influence, particularly in the context of Schiavo's case and its aftermath. This

---

[12] For one illustration of this debate, see Thomas A. Shannon and James J. Walter, "Assisted Nutrition and Hydration and the Catholic Tradition," *Theological Studies* 66, no. 3 (2005): 651–662; John J. Paris, James F. Keenan, and Kenneth R. Himes, "*Quaestio Disputata*: Did John Paul II's Allocution on Life-Sustaining Treatments Revise Tradition?" *Theological Studies* 67, no. 1 (2006): 163–168; Thomas A. Shannon and James J. Walter, "A Reply to Professors Paris, Keenan, and Himes," *Theological Studies* 67, no. 1 (2006): 169–174. See also Kevin O'Rourke, "Reflections on the Papal Allocution Concerning Care for Persistent Vegetative State Patients," *Christian Bioethics* 12, no. 1 (2006): 83–97. For a thorough account of how this debated question was treated before the papal allocution, see Michael R. Panicola, "Withdrawing Nutrition and Hydration," *Health Progress* 82, no. 6 (2001): 28–33.

[13] Congregation for the Doctrine of the Faith, "Responses to Certain Questions of the United States Conference of Catholic Bishops Concerning Artificial Nutrition and Hydration," September 16, 2007, www.vatican.va/roman_curia/congregations/cfaith/documents/rc_con_cfaith_doc_20070801_risposte-usa_en.html; Congregation for the Doctrine of the Faith, "Commentary on Responses to Questions Presented by His Excellency the Most Reverend William S. Skylstad," August 1, 2007, www.vatican.va/roman_curia/congregations/cfaith/documents/rc_con_cfaith_doc_20070801_nota-commento_en.html. See also Ron Hamel, "The CDF Statement on Artificial Nutrition and Hydration: What Should We Make of It?," *Health Care Ethics USA* 15, no. 4 (2007): 5–7; Kevin D. O'Rourke and John J. Hardt, "Nutrition and Hydration: The CDF Response, in Perspective," *Health Progress* 88, no. 6 (2007): 44–47; Justin F. Rigali and William E. Lori, "On Basic Care for Patients in the 'Vegetative State:' A Response to Dr. Hardt and Fr. O'Rourke," *Health Progress* 89, no. 3 (2008): 70–72.

[14] For an overview of the way this case unfolded in the culture wars, see Cathleen Kaveny, *Prophecy without Contempt: Religious Discourse in the Public Square* (Cambridge: Harvard University Press, 2016), 65–74.

[15] James T. Bretzke, "A Burden of Means: Interpreting Recent Catholic Magisterial Teaching on End-of-Life Issues," *Journal of the Society of Christian Ethics* 26, no. 2 (2006): 183–200.

result is especially troubling because, as the debate over Schiavo's case illustrates, an abstract determination of a particular treatment as an ordinary means restricts the work of grace to the attempt to prolong temporal life.

Admittedly, few of the people discussing Schiavo's case appealed to the work of grace, but the public discourse from Catholic leaders at the time reveals implicit assumptions about the place of grace at the end of life. The best example is a statement from Archbishop Charles Chaput, then head of the Archdiocese of Denver, who condemned the removal of Schiavo's feeding tube as "a form of murder...[that] attack[s] the sanctity of human life...[and] reject[s] any redemptive meaning to suffering."[16] By appealing to the affront to the sanctity of human life, Chaput's statement implied that the grace of life was not appropriately recognized and honored in Schiavo's case. At the same time, by lamenting the dismissal of suffering's redemptive meaning, his statement also suggested that the removal of Schiavo's feeding tube was a missed opportunity for grace, leaving one to infer that the real place to search for grace at the end of life is in the divine assistance necessary to persevere in the face of exceptionally challenging medical conditions, no matter how debilitating. Other Catholic leaders, including Cardinal Renato Martino, the head of the Pontifical Council for Justice and Peace at the time, made similarly strong statements.[17]

Of course, there are a number of unique issues in Schiavo's case, and the discussion here is not meant to gloss over the complexities involved, but it is important to appeal to this example nonetheless because the very public debate about Schiavo's treatment ensured that a certain interpretation of Catholic teaching on end-of-life care managed to shape the narrative of the day.[18] Reflecting on the case and the larger duty to preserve life, the senior ethicist for the Catholic Health Association at the time, Ron Hamel, noted that

> Two standards for making decisions about nutrition and hydration have emerged and now exist side by side. One is a more holistic standard based on the traditional teaching, in which benefits and burdens

---

[16] Charles J. Chaput, "Statement by Archbishop Chaput on Terri Schiavo," *Catholic News Agency*, March 22, 2005, www.catholicnewsagency.com/document/statement-by-archbishop-chaput-on-terri-schiavo-252.

[17] Renato R. Martino, "Statement of Cardinal Renato Martino on Behalf of Terri Schiavo," *Catholic Culture*, March 7, 2005, www.catholicculture.org/culture/library/view.cfm?recnum=6374.

[18] Kaveny makes the point that the contributions of leading Catholics to the popular debate were mainly in the form of prophetic rhetoric and as such presumed that their interpretation of the moral obligations in the case was the only possible interpretation that could be sustained by people who shared their same religious and moral commitments, see Kaveny, *Prophecy without Contempt*, 71–72.

are understood broadly relative to the person, and any means of preserving life is subject to a benefit-burden analysis. The other is a more restrictive standard based on recent revisions of the traditional teaching, in which benefits and burdens are understood narrowly, apart from relative factors, and nutrition and hydration are given a special moral classification.[19]

Although Hamel demurred on which of these two standards was taking hold (notably, he wrote while Schiavo's case was still unfolding), Thomas Shannon and James Walter were more insistent after witnessing the concerted Catholic response to Schiavo's situation, offering, "we remain persuaded that there is…a shift to deontological reasoning in the area of death and dying, complemented by categorizing interventions as ordinary or extraordinary [in isolation]."[20] They pointed directly to John Paul II's 2004 allocution as the tipping point.

There is much to suggest that Shannon and Walter are right: there has been a shift toward deontological thinking in the approach to death and dying. On the one hand, there were a number of cultural factors that encouraged this shift, most notably concerns about the contemporaneous movement seeking to legalize euthanasia and physician assisted suicide.[21] Against this background, the impulse is certainly understandable. On the other hand, there are real costs to this development. The greatest cost is in the growing assumption among ordinary Catholics that they must do everything in their power to fight death for themselves and their loved ones or else they risk turning into unconscious pawns in the culture of death, actively involved in violating the sanctity of human life as a gift from God. However dramatic this may sound, personal anecdotal evidence reveals there are people facing these sorts of end-of-life decisions who earnestly feel this way. Often, many of them are led to this conclusion by their well-meaning parish priests who have followed the public battles over end-of-life care for Catholics but have not had the opportunity to delve into the particulars of the church's long tradition.[22]

---

[19] Ronald Hamel, "Must We Preserve Life?," *America*, April 19, 2004, www.americamagazine.org/issue/482/article/must-we-preserve-life.
[20] Shannon and Walter, "A Reply," 173.
[21] See Michael D. Place, "Thoughts on the Papal Allocution," *Health Progress* 85, no. 4 (2004): 6, 60.
[22] In recognition of precisely this challenge, Catholic Health Association USA has launched a series of workshops for clergy to familiarize them with the details of the church's position on end-of-life care. One part of the workshop is dedicated to "dispelling myths," specifically the "misconception that the Catholic Church requires Catholics to say yes to all medical interventions." Julie Minda, "Clergy Gain Insights on Assisting in End-of-Life Care Choices," *Catholic Health World*, May 15, 2018, www.chausa.org/publications/catholic-health-world/archives/issues/may-15-2018/clergy-gain-insights-on-assisting-in-end-of-life-care-choices.

If all this led to merely a presumption in favor of something like artificial nutrition and hydration—which the USCCB's *Ethical and Religious Directives* (ERDs) affirms—then one might be tempted to say no harm, no foul.[23] The problem, however, is that this logic is not restricted to artificial nutrition and hydration but is instead applied to interventions more broadly. People begin to think that the only way to cooperate with grace at the end of life is to fight for life and to hope for the grace to persevere through suffering in that fight.

Of course, this is not to say that people only come to this conclusion as a result of Catholic involvement in the culture wars. There are other cultural influences at work, especially the "idolatry of health" and the growing assumption that the purpose of modern medicine is to eliminate suffering and, ideally, counteract the effects of mortality.[24] The net effect of these developments, though, is that questions of the proportionate and disproportionate nature of certain means have begun to disappear, except for the most well-informed patient, and Catholics have instead defaulted in favor of intervention. Given the history of the principle of ordinary and extraordinary means, this is a theological problem because of what it says about our appreciation of grace, and it is also a pastoral problem for the stress it adds to families at an especially trying time. Just as importantly, this change is also a theological problem because of what it does to the distribution of scarce medical resources.

THE EXTRAORDINARY NATURE OF ORDINARY MEANS IN A GLOBAL CONTEXT

The narrowing of options for faithful Catholics and the implicit restriction of grace to the active fight to preserve life presents poignant problems in light of contemporary health care disparities. As the physician and reformer Paul Farmer is quick to point out, the story of medicine in the contemporary world is a story of radical disparities, all of which revolve around one feature: poverty. "Surveys have shown," Farmer notes in an article with his colleague Nicole Gastineau Campos, "that in the world's poorest countries, the affluent have ready access to [expensive modern medical treatments like]...antiretroviral agents...therapy for renal insufficiency...[and] NICUs.... At the same time, the world's poor, even those living in wealthy nations, do not have reliable access to good medical care or to the fruits

---

[23] United States Conference of Catholic Bishops, *Ethical and Religious Directives for Catholic Health Care Services*, 5th ed. (Washington, DC: United States Conference of Catholic Bishops, 2009), no. 58; cf. Shannon and Walter, "A Reply," 172.

[24] George Khushf, "Illness, the Problem of Evil, and the Analogical Structure of Healing: On the Difference Christianity Makes in Bioethics," *Christian Bioethics* 1, no. 1 (1995): 102–120; Stanley Hauerwas, *Naming the Silences: God, Medicine, and the Problem of Suffering* (London: T&T Clark, 2004), 101.

of medical science."²⁵ This truth is readily apparent to anyone who has seen understaffed inner-city trauma centers in the United States or who has traveled abroad to oppressed areas of the global south.

Nevertheless, Catholic health care ethics has not grappled with this reality effectively. As Daniel Daly observed in his own work contextualizing the ethics of end-of-life care in a world of radical health inequities, "While the suffering and premature death that is commonplace in the global south has emerged as a central topic within Catholic medical ethics, few moral conclusions have changed as a result. The diminished and shortened lives of the global poor are lamented but have not concretely altered moral analysis or conclusions."²⁶ Undoubtedly, this reality is something that end-of-life ethics needs to take more seriously, and the application of the principle of ordinary and extraordinary means should not be immune to this global reality.

To give a quick sense of the problem in more concrete terms, consider just a few sobering statistics. Less than a decade ago, the World Health Organization reported that OECD countries consumed 86 percent of all health dollars spent globally while encompassing only 18 percent of the population.²⁷ Unsurprisingly, this translates into significant disparities in access to health care services, and the WHO estimates that even today "at least half of the world's population cannot obtain essential health services."²⁸ A number of examples reveal very clearly that this half of the world's population is defined by poverty and, by extension, geography since truly abject poverty is concentrated in the so-called developing nations of the global south. First, a 2010 review of trends in maternal mortality found that 99% of all women who died from complications related to their pregnancy lived in developing nations.²⁹ Second, the leading cause of "lost life years" (i.e., early death) in the global north and BRICS nations (Brazil, Russia, India, China, and South Africa) is almost universally heart disease, a tricky medical problem to address. The leading cause of lost life

---

[25] Paul Farmer and Nicole Gastineau Campos, "Rethinking Medical Ethics: A View from Below," *Developing World Bioethics* 4, no. 1 (2004): 17–41.

[26] Daniel J. Daly, "Unreasonable Means: Proposing a New Category for Catholic End-of-Life Ethics," *Christian Bioethics* 19, no. 1 (2013): 46.

[27] World Health Organization, *The World Health Report: Health Systems Financing: The Path to Universal Coverage* (Geneva: WHO Press, 2010), 4. Available online at www.who.int/whr/2010/en/.

[28] World Health Organization, "World Bank and WHO: Half the World Lacks Access to Essential Health Services, 100 Million Still Pushed into Extreme Poverty because of Health Expenses," December 13, 2017, www.who.int/en/news-room/detail/13-12-2017-world-bank-and-who-half-the-world-lacks-access-to-essential-health-services-100-million-still-pushed-into-extreme-poverty-because-of-health-expenses.

[29] World Health Organization, *Trends in Maternal Mortality: 1990 to 2010* (Geneva: WHO Press, 2012), 22. Available online at apps.who.int/iris/bitstream/handle/10665/44874/9789241503631_eng.pdf?sequence=1.

years in the global south, however, runs the gamut from HIV/AIDS (similarly tricky to tackle, yet with a clearer management plan than heart disease) to malaria, diarrhea, and pneumonia-type illnesses, which have much less costly solutions.[30] Third, as Paul Farmer helpfully illustrated in the midst of the 2013–2016 Ebola outbreak, most health care disparities today come down to the distribution of "staff, space, stuff, and systems." The varying availability (or unavailability) of these four things explains why Ebola mortality rates hovered at 75% in Western African nations but plateaued at 25% in Germany during a rare outbreak there *nearly half a century earlier*.[31] This gets to the heart of the problem, revealing that global health care disparities are chiefly about access to care and that the worst of these disparities reflects the lack of access to even basic medical care that the WHO has ascribed to at least one half of the world's population.

In a world where the majority of people cannot reliably hope to receive everyday health care treatments like vaccines, prenatal monitoring, and safe drinking water, surely one has to reconsider what constitutes an ordinary means of preserving life. Admittedly, this is not an easy thing to do. The traditional approach to ordinary and extraordinary means has presumed that these categories need to accommodate local variation, since the means in question have to be available to a given patient in his or her particular situation.[32] The CDF's initial interpretation of John Paul II's allocution follows this logic in asserting a permissible exception to the obligation to provide artificial nutrition and hydration "in very remote places or in situations of extreme poverty…[where] the artificial provision of food and water may be physically impossible."[33] The prevailing norm, however, is that treatments normally accessible in one part of the world ought to be identified as ordinary means—and thus obligatory interventions, all things being equal—for all patients in the same locale, except when medical futility arises in particular cases. There are good reasons for this norm because it militates against disparate treatment of similar patients in the same context and bolsters the argument for providing an equally rigorous standard of care to all patients as a matter of justice.

Unfortunately, this approach also masks and exacerbates global health inequities because it encourages people to take a local view of their place in an increasingly interconnected health care infrastructure.

---

[30] Dylan Matthews, "The #1 Reason People Die Early, in Each Country," *Vox*, March 13, 2015, www.vox.com/2015/1/2/7474995/map-years-lost-life.
[31] Jonathan Hiskes, "Stopping Infectious Disease Requires 'Staff, Space, Stuff, and Systems,' Paul Farmer Argues," *Medium*, February 20, 2018, medium.com/@simpsoncenter/stopping-infectious-disease-requires-staff-space-stuff-and-systems-paul-farmer-argues-with-8f59e5ad79d4.
[32] Pope Pius XII, "The Prolongation of Life," 94.
[33] Congregation for the Doctrine of the Faith, "Commentary."

When people evaluate the benefits and burdens of a proposed treatment in the narrow context of their place in the United States, for instance, they can quickly overlook the fact that this treatment might be very costly, contributing to the disproportionate use of health care resources in the global north and thereby undermining the expansion of access to basic care in the global south. Granted, this is not strictly the result of a direct causal chain, although in a globalized world with finite health care resources, overuse by some still does result in underuse by others. The strongest impact arises from the creation of misaligned incentives, such as the way that the rich health care markets of the global north prompt a "brain drain" from the global south as trained medical professionals seek higher paying jobs and better working conditions in wealthier countries, creating shortages of health care workers in their homelands.[34] In light of these challenges, it is necessary to encourage a greater sense of (global) solidarity in the ethical discernment surrounding end-of-life care.

Of course, this is not exactly a novel suggestion. In the early 2000s, Lisa Sowle Cahill made the case for a theological approach to health care ethics that would distinguish itself, in part, from its secular counterparts by its explicit emphasis on evaluating bioethics as a social ethics issue.[35] One of the ways she illustrated this approach was with a powerful critique of the tendency to use a concern for the vulnerable as an excuse to ignore the impact of end-of-life care on the common good. Pointing toward the implications of a more globally-conscious perspective, Cahill argued that "specific allocations of health care resources need to be made...in awareness of the need for redistributive justice in meeting basic needs of persons in less advantaged societies before providing relatively expensive or exotic life-prolonging technologies to those in more privileged circumstances."[36] The present effort to reexamine ordinary and extraordinary means adds specificity to some of Cahill's critiques and extends her concerns, many of which have only been amplified by the global rise in inequality that has been

---

[34] Daly, "Unreasonable Means," 48. This can also be seen in the way that the outsized scope of the U.S. drug market orients research and development toward the inconveniences of an aging population (e.g., erectile dysfunction) and away from the life-threatening problems of the global population (e.g., malaria). Conor M. Kelly, "Pharmaceutical Development and Structural Sin: Diagnosing and Confronting Global Health Care Disparities," presented at the Catholic Theology Society of America Annual Convention, Milwaukee, WI, June 11–14, 2015.
[35] Lisa Sowle Cahill, *Theological Bioethics: Participation, Justice, Change* (Washington, DC: Georgetown University Press, 2005), 1–3.
[36] Cahill, *Theological Bioethics*, 110.

a defining feature of the last thirteen years since her book was published.[37]

While Cahill set the stage, in many ways, for a more globally conscious approach to health care ethics in general, another theological ethicist has followed her lead to address end-of-life care specifically from the perspective of social ethics. Writing with an acute awareness of global health disparities, the aforementioned Daniel Daly proposed a solution to the disproportionate use of health care resources for end-of-life care in developed countries by championing the addition of a new category to the principle of ordinary and extraordinary means that would create "an upper moral limit on medical treatment at the end of life."[38] His concept of "unreasonable means" (a term borrowed from David Kelly) prohibits the use of treatments "when the burdens to the patient and community far outpace the benefits to the patient...and when [their] use...directly or indirectly limits another patient's access to ordinary means."[39] This is an important development that goes a long way in addressing the myopia that the culturally variable account of ordinary and extraordinary means promotes. It highlights the interrelated nature of health care decisions in a world of finite health care resources, and it invites the cultivation of solidarity as a patient or a patient's family begins to consider personal medical decisions in relation to the common good. Precisely for these reasons, Daly's solution serves an essential function in contemporary health care ethics, and it represents a necessary addition to Catholic end-of-life ethics in particular. However necessary, though, Daly's category of unreasonable means is not sufficient alone. Given the recent developments in assumptions regarding the principle of ordinary and extraordinary means, the problem of inordinate uses of health care resources cannot be solved solely by adding to the distinction in order to expand its force. Instead, the distinction itself needs reevaluation.

The solution proposed here, then, is to take Daly's instincts and apply them to the other end of the spectrum of care. Daly offers a terminus at one end by arguing that unreasonable means are morally prohibited. This leaves ordinary means as the morally obligatory way to prolong life and extraordinary means as the morally supererogatory (i.e., optional) way to prolong life. If one considers things in these terms, it is easy to see how the distinction itself contributes to the problem, especially when the category of ordinary means begins to balloon to encompass more interventions less critically. To be more precise, the rapid expansion of the category of ordinary means has facilitated

---

[37] For more on the increasing prevalence of inequality worldwide and its ethical implications, see Kate Ward and Kenneth R. Himes, "'Growing Apart': The Rise of Inequality," *Theological Studies* 75, no. 1 (2014): 118–132.
[38] Daly, "Unreasonable Means," 52.
[39] Daly, "Unreasonable Means," 52–53.

broader trends, like the medicalization of human health and the expanding vision of medicine's proper purpose, which lead to the disproportionate use of health care resources in developed nations like the United States, because the category tells Catholics that they must use certain treatment options at the end of life. Given that end-of-life care is one of the most expensive categories of care, this perspective certainly has the potential to exacerbate the current global health inequities.[40] In response, Catholic health care ethics needs to find a way to give greater latitude to the interpretation of ordinary means, thereby counteracting the implicit narrowing of the space for grace in end-of-life care that has accompanied the rise of deontological thinking in the application of the principle of ordinary and extraordinary means.

In concrete terms, this solution entails an expansion of the factors that ought to be evaluated when one employs the principle of ordinary and extraordinary means to discern appropriate end-of-life care. Currently, "places, times, and culture" are a factor in the determination of ordinary means, and this is quite appropriate for the reasons outlined above. Yet, in a world of global health care disparities, it is not enough to see the distinction between ordinary and extraordinary means in a local context alone. As a matter of solidarity, which involves "a firm and persevering commitment to the common good; that is to say to the good of all and of each individual, because we are all really responsible for all" (*Sollicitudo Rei Socialis*, no. 38), Catholics ought also to consider the ways that access to care affects the determination of ordinary means. More specifically, they need to account for the fact that what is ordinary in a U.S. context might be deemed quite extraordinary in much of the rest of the world. The best way to do this is to discern the burdens of a proposed treatment not simply in one's immediate circumstances but also according to a broader global perspective.

Something along these lines is already presumed in the work of discerning ordinary and extraordinary means, for as the ERDs summarize that long tradition, ordinary means "are those that in the judgment of the patient offer a reasonable hope of benefit and do not entail an excessive burden or impose excessive expense on the family or the community."[41] By highlighting the need to consider not simply the burdens to the patient himself or herself but also to the larger circles of family and community, the ERDs present the principle of ordinary

---

[40] Studies of the U.S. Medicare system indicate that nearly one-third of all Medicare expenditures go to the five percent of patients who die in a given year. Amber E. Barnato, Mark B. McClellan, Christopher R. Kagay, and Alan M. Garber, "Trends in Inpatient Treatment Intensity among Beneficiaries at the End of Life," *Health Services Research* 39, no. 2 (2004): 364.

[41] United States Conference of Catholic Bishops, *Ethical and Religious Directives*, no. 56.

and extraordinary means as a potential tool of solidarity insofar as it invites the patient to see herself or himself as a person in relationship with others whose wellbeing is also a concern. The challenge, though, is that this broader sense of burden is often hard to gauge, especially since each person is a constituent of multiple communities. The point of this proposal, then, is to invite patients to recognize themselves as members of the global community and to encourage them to account for the burdens their treatment(s) might impose on that community as well. Given the disproportionate use of health care resources by the global north and the misaligned incentives that this reality creates, patients in a U.S. context should address their global accountability by assessing the extent to which a proposed treatment reinforces international disparities by using resources to provide a form of care in the global north that is inaccessible to the majority of the population in the global south.

In practical terms, one can envision this type of discernment as a twofold process. First, a patient would evaluate the benefits and burdens of a treatment according to her or his immediate circumstances. Then, the patient would try to imagine how he or she would evaluate the benefits and burdens of the same treatment if he or she were in another part of the world, like the global south, focusing on the additional burdens and new obstacles that might stand in the way of treatment when one can no longer count on the advantages of a well-established health care system. In many instances, this twofold process would likely generate some degree of dissonance, for the unjust distribution of health care resources, which results in lower standards of care in the global south, could very well lead to the conclusion that what a patient discerns as an ordinary treatment in the United States is deemed extraordinary by the majority of the world's population. The obvious question is what a patient ought to do with this dissonance, and this is where the Catholic moral tradition's insistence that the determination of an ordinary or extraordinary means can only occur in the concrete situation of a patient's particular course of treatment becomes especially important, for it indicates that the resolution of this dissonance is a matter of conscience.[42] While this may seem flippant or dismissive, it is not. As "the most secret core and sanctuary of a [human person where one]...is alone with God, Whose voice echoes in his [or her] depths" (*Gaudium et Spes*, no. 16), conscience is precisely where this decision should take place, for the final determination of whether one's end-of-life care represents an ordinary or extraordinary means comes down to discerning how one is called to cooperate with God's grace.

---

[42] James T. Bretzke, "Ordinary and Extraordinary Means," in *A Handbook of Roman Catholic Moral Terms* (Washington, DC: Georgetown University Press, 2013), 167–168.

While the ultimate decision remains a matter of conscience, which always operates in the concrete and cannot be predetermined,[43] attention to the work of grace at the end of life suggests that certain outcomes might be more common than others. Specifically, one can imagine that in most cases the twofold discernment process would still lead patients to accept treatment as an ordinary means according to their local context. This is because adequate respect for the sanctity of life as a gift of grace justifies deference to a more expansive definition of ordinary means, which is typically going to arise from the local rather than the global analysis. Even in these instances, though, it will still be helpful for patients to have examined their decision from a global perspective, for this can promote an appropriate sense of global awareness that better enables one to appreciate both the fragility of life as a gift of grace and the privilege of cooperating with grace in its preservation. In some unique cases, though, the disconnect between local and global understandings of ordinary means might prompt a particular patient to forgo a treatment that he or she initial discerned to be an ordinary means of prolonging life in his or her locale, as long he or she did so under narrow circumstances and for the right reasons. This, of course, is where the greatest impact of this twofold discernment process comes to light, for it represents a departure from the typical assumptions surrounding the principle of ordinary and extraordinary means. Currently, the local decision is the one that creates the force of moral obligation, for that which a patient discerns to be an ordinary means according to his or her time, place, and culture must, for that very reason, be used to prolong the patient's life. With the addition of a global perspective, however, the obligation can give way to a concern for global justice, which is consistent with both the Christian understanding of the practical implications of faith in Jesus Christ as the Son of God and, as outlined below, the belief that God's grace is at work in the world, even at the end of life.[44]

Before addressing the opportunities for grace inherent in this new approach to ordinary and extraordinary means, it seems prudent to offer a bit more detail about the unique areas where a patient's judgment of conscience might prompt them to defer to the discernment of extraordinary means according to the global rather than local perspective. While it is tempting to try to articulate a set of criteria that would restrict this situation in advance, such an approach would merely perpetuate some of the problems that have given rise to the need for a

---

[43] Timothy O'Connell, *Principles for a Catholic Morality*, Revised Edition (New York: Harper Collins, 1990), 112.

[44] For a robust defense of the compatibility of a commitment to global justice with Christian faith, see Lisa Sowle Cahill, *Global Justice, Christology, and Christian Ethics* (Cambridge: Cambridge University Press, 2003).

new interpretation of ordinary and extraordinary means in the first place. After all, the twofold process proposed here is designed, in part, to counteract the tendency to view ordinary means as a deontological category. Fortunately, the well-established tradition of moral discernment through casuistry offers a way to develop some additional specificity without devolving into a deontological calculus. Consider, then, the case of patients in a persistent vegetative state, which is, of course, the question that has been at the heart of the very deontological shift that needs more critical evaluation.

In this case, the twofold discernment process articulated above entails that a Catholic could, in good conscience, instruct his or her health care proxy to discontinue artificial nutrition and hydration if he or she were diagnosed in a persistent vegetative state (and had been in that state for a sufficiently prolonged period virtually to eliminate the possibility of eventual recovery). In this situation, the Catholic in question would need to settle on these instructions not out of a fear of being stuck in this life in this condition but out of a desire to avoid excessively taxing the health care system in a way that perpetuates the disproportionate use of medical resources in the global north (as a whole) and encourages the persistence of the global health care system's perverse incentives. In a word, this would have to be a selfless decision, motivated by the recognition that in many—in fact, most—parts of the world this diagnosis would be an almost immediate death sentence because even the relatively rudimentary care of continual nursing and artificial nutrition and hydration is inaccessible. Out of solidarity with the majority of the population in this situation and out of a desire to combat the very inequities that make this lack of access a reality, one in this context could opt out of the active interventions of the modern health care system and instead ask for hospice care so that there might be additional resources available for more basic (or perhaps similarly basic) care for more people in the world. Granted, the act would likely be one of prophetic resistance to a large-scale structural problem rather than a direct solution to it, but the example of Jesus clearly shows that there is value—and more importantly, grace—in these kinds of actions. While this discernment might seem to contradict the official magisterial interpretation of artificial nutrition and hydration, observers who are attuned to the intricacies of magisterial authority and papal pronouncements note that the Magisterium's "official" position on artificial nutrition and hydration (even for patients in a persistent vegetative state) is not so clear cut.[45] Consequently, the effect of the twofold discernment process advocated here is not to contradict magisterial teaching but to nuance its interpretation and application, so that an isolated reading of one papal address does not undercut the Catholic community's fidelity to its core

---

[45] Bretzke, "A Burden of Means," 195.

convictions like hope for the resurrection or a commitment to the preferential option for the poor.

Naturally, there are likely to be concerns with an approach like this, especially since one of the factors motivating the shift toward a deontological interpretation of ordinary and extraordinary means was a desire to protect life at all of its vulnerable stages. While this is a laudable goal, it is important to recognize that expanding the notion of ordinary means in a *prima facie* fashion does not serve this end directly. Certainly, as suggested above, a tendency to categorize a specific medical treatment as an ordinary means of prolonging life can aid the effort to insist that every patient should, as a matter of justice, have access to that treatment, but the notion of ordinary means does not directly entail this conclusion. The real moral implication of defining something as an ordinary means is not that everyone should have access to this means of preserving life but that anyone who does have access must use it. On its own, the principle of ordinary and extraordinary means is not about access to care, which is why patients and their families need to be encouraged to incorporate a broader perspective when they apply this principle. The global perspective presented here as part of a twofold discernment process does this by creating more space for the exercise of conscience in the adjudication of ordinary means. Thus, the notion of a broader process that compares local determinations with global realities prompts a question of justice and might lead to different choices, which, collectively, could have the power to undo some of the injustices plaguing health care today. Of course, this appeal to conscience carries risks of relativism alongside the risk that a patient or his or her family might make a morally bad decision, but such is the nature of conscience in fallible human beings. The Catholic community ought to be willing to accept these risks in order to honor the high dignity of conscience. Furthermore, the Catholic community ought to tolerate these risks out of a respect for the dynamism of grace because the incorporation of a global perspective in end-of-life discernment invites a new openness to all the possibilities of grace at the end of life.

At the moment, as explained above, the common interpretation of grace at the end of life is limited. Despite the fact that the principle of ordinary and extraordinary means points to grace at both of its poles, the application of this principle has led to the assumption that the proper place to search for grace is with the patient who insists on fighting to the end, despite any suffering, so that she or he can enjoy the grace of a purely "natural death." In this model, there is little space for grace in the patient who chooses to forgo or to cease treatments that could prolong life but not change the inevitable. Such a person seems to be giving up at precisely the moment he or she is called to be

Grace at the End of Life   107

ramping up for battle instead. Yet surely grace is not so restrictive. The very gratuity of grace suggests that God's love cannot be confined in advance. Fortunately, the introduction of a global perspective provides a theological explanation of the ways that grace can be operative not only in the choice to battle for one's life but also in the decision to accept one's finitude in a way that springs from a concern for others. Here a Rahnerian notion of grace is especially informative, for Karl Rahner described grace as God's self-communication, or agapic gift of self, to the world.[46] Hence, he identified the experience of grace as self-transcendence, specifically the form of transcendence that allows one to move beyond self-concern to a selfless concern for others.[47] Insofar as a patient chooses, after an appropriately careful discernment process, to forgo what they discern to be a locally ordinary but globally extraordinary treatment out of a selfless concern for others' ability to access care—especially a selfless concern for the poor's ability to access care—then that patient is necessarily a recipient and a conduit of grace in the world, for there is in Rahnerian terms no other explanation for this agapic gift of self than the gift of God's very essence, *agape*, grace. If Catholic health care ethics has no way to countenance this decision, then Catholics might very well be led astray in their search for grace at the end of life.

To be clear, no part of this defense of a twofold approach to ordinary and extraordinary means is meant to suggest that every person should use this perspective to forgo any and all end of life treatments. The point, instead, is to carve out room for Catholic ethics to acknowledge more explicitly that a Catholic in good conscience *could* take this route, at least under certain circumstances. With its greater flexibility for consciences, the twofold discernment process outlined here allows the principle of ordinary and extraordinary means to account better for the pitfalls of this present, imperfect world and also to acknowledge more readily the multifaceted nature of grace's forays into that same present, imperfect world.

This approach will not, however, solve everything. In fact, the introduction of a global perspective is much more of a bandage than a cure. The end goal must be to expand access to care so that there would be less need for a twofold discernment process because the burdens of receiving the same treatment will be distributed less unevenly across the globe. A process of double discernment serves this goal by raising awareness about the problem and by reminding people of the ways that their seemingly private decisions always have social ramifications

---

[46] Karl Rahner, *Foundations of the Christian Faith: An Introduction to the Idea of Christianity*, trans. William V. Dych (New York: Seabury Press, 1978), 116–117.
[47] Karl Rahner, "Reflections on the Experience of Grace," in *Theological Investigations, Volume Three*, trans. Karl-H. Kruger and Boniface Kruger (Baltimore: Helicon, 1965), 89.

in a world of finite resources. Still, individual recognition of this interconnectedness will not suddenly fix the unjust distribution of health care goods. Real change will only come as a result of reforms in the social, political, and economic structures that constrain choices and perpetuate injustices—that is, through transformation of the structures of sin underlying the global health care system today.[48]

Such structural changes are, however, impossible to imagine without a committed group of personal moral agents whose consciences are attuned to the magnitude of the problem at hand. Hence, the global approach to end-of-life care defended here might best be described as a necessary but not sufficient condition for the rectification of the global injustices in access to health care. Significantly, even this small step in the right direction will be difficult to achieve because there are other structural pressures that militate against even a limited conscientization like this. Additional changes will surely be necessary before more people can make the globally-conscious discernment of ordinary and extraordinary means envisioned here. By way of conclusion, then, this paper closes with a brief discussion of two of the changes that might set the stage for a better embrace of the global approach to ordinary and extraordinary means.

MAKING GLOBAL EVALUATION A REALITY

Certainly, there are obstacles that stand in the way of greater global awareness in health care, especially in the United States. There are many forms of moral inertia, both personal and institutional, that are already working to frustrate this more nuanced form of moral discernment. Among the many examples one might imagine, two are prominent enough to merit attention as a fitting conclusion to the argument for the global approach to end-of-life care.

The first illustration of the inertia standing in the way of a global approach to ordinary and extraordinary means is personal. People have been primed to view health care as an eminently personal choice, and they are encouraged to make their health care decisions with their own self-interest in mind. People want the best care possible for themselves, and they will positively insist upon it for their family members (especially if those family members are minors). This is a natural instinct, and morally speaking it is also a healthy one, for it respects the Thomistic ordering of charity, which acknowledges responsibilities for one's own well-being (ST II-II, q. 26, a. 4) and also delineates varying degrees of obligation to one's neighbor according to familial

---

[48] For more on structures of sin and their effects, see Finn, "What is a Sinful Social Structure?" 136–164. Pope Francis also points specifically to the role of "unjust social structures" in the perpetuation of inequality (*Evangelii Gaudium*, no. 59).

bonds, among other things (ST II-II, q. 26, a. 7–8).[49] Furthermore, there are virtuous interpretations of this instinct, especially when one thinks of James Keenan's relational account of the cardinal virtues, which promotes both self-care and fidelity as good dispositions for the moral life.[50] Nevertheless, this instinct must not become absolute. Christianity has, for millennia, used the words and example of Jesus to criticize an exclusive prioritization of kin responsibilities, insisting instead that the sphere of moral responsibility cannot be limited to ties of blood alone.[51] Keenan's system of virtues, meanwhile, notes that the obligations of self-care and fidelity have to be weighed, with the assistance of prudence, against the demands of justice.[52] Unfortunately, as the struggle to incorporate both of these insights into ordinary moral discernment illustrates, there is a considerable gap between admitting this moral responsibility and actually living it out in practice. Before a global approach to ordinary and extraordinary means can hope to have any impact, it will need to address this gap.

The best way to challenge the gap, and thereby to make the global perspective more influential in ethical discernment at the end of life, is to promote the cultivation of solidarity throughout the entirety of one's life. As both the descriptive fact of human interconnectedness and the spirit of moral obligation that flows from that fact, solidarity has the potential to impact ethical discernment in a profound and encompassing way.[53] As Pope Francis explained, solidarity "refers to something more than a few sporadic acts of generosity. It presumes the creation of a new mindset which thinks in terms of community and the priority of the life of all over the appropriation of goods by a few" (*Evangelii Gaudium*, no. 187). In an individualistic society like the United States, though, this is far from a natural instinct.[54] Consequently, if the ultimate aim is to have more Catholics engaging in the twofold discernment process proposed here as an act of solidarity then Catholics first need to be encouraged to practice solidarity in more

---

[49] Strikingly, kinship bonds are so important in Aquinas' conception of the ordering of charity that he dedicates a series of articles to adjudicating one's responsibilities to various family members (ST II-II, q. 26, a. 9–11).
[50] James F. Keenan, S.J., "Proposing Cardinal Virtues," *Theological Studies* 56, no. 4 (1995): 709–729.
[51] See Julie Hanlon Rubio, *A Christian Theology of Marriage and Family* (New York: Paulist Press, 2003), 49–54.
[52] Keenan, "Proposing Cardinal Virtues," 724, 728.
[53] Gerald J. Beyer, "The Meaning of Solidarity in Catholic Social Teaching," *Political Theology* 15, no. 1 (2014): 7–25.
[54] By virtually any measure, the United States is one of the most individualistic countries in the world. A famous study of "culture and organizations" by Dutch psychologist and anthropologist Geert Hofstede placed the United States at the top of the list of individualistic cultures. Geert Hofstede, Gert Jan Hofstede, Michael Minkov, *Cultures and Organizations: Software of the Mind; Intercultural Cooperation and Its Importance for Survival*, Third Edition (New York: McGraw Hill, 2010), 93–95.

routine matters of ethical discernment. Then, they will be prepared to use solidarity as a central guiding feature in their major ethical decisions, like the discernment of ordinary and extraordinary forms of end-of-life care.

To give just a few examples of how this cultivation of an everyday form of solidarity might occur, a parish could organize a talk on *Laudato Si'* and then hand out shower timers at the end as a way of prompting the faithful to recognize that water is a finite resource in the world, even if it is not in their local community. People could be encouraged to put their phones away during their free time so that they might build relationships rather than feed into the isolating tendencies of an increasingly technology-saturated culture.[55] This could occur by championing public goods, like city parks, over private ones, like country clubs, so that people might build connections to their community as a whole and not just to individual friends in isolation.[56]

These examples, though, are merely the beginning. The message needs to be that the work of solidarity never ends, and, therefore, that every ethical choice should be made with an awareness of its impact on others. In this way, the local church can work to ensure that the valorization of individualism and personal autonomy might not hold the same sway on the faithful Catholic that it holds on people in the United States more generally. Given the force of individualism as a cultural value, the everyday development of solidarity is the only way that Catholics in the United States can be expected to see the global perspective on ordinary and extraordinary means as a genuine invitation to explore the role of grace in their lives and not as an external imposition encroaching on their individual rights.

In the absence of this development, a global consciousness will be an unrealistic ideal, especially for the majority of U.S. Catholics. The appropriate pastoral response, then, would not be to give up on the twofold process of discernment entirely but rather to underscore the importance of evaluating community burdens in the assessment of ordinary and extraordinary means and to encourage patients to think of their social responsibilities in progressively larger senses. This might allow them to imagine how the burdens of their treatment would look different if they were in a less well-connected area of the United States or if they had fewer economic resources but were in the same location. In this way, the twofold discernment process could still promote a sense of solidarity with those in need, and it could still call attention

---

[55] See Sherry Turkle, *Alone Together: Why We Expect More from Technology and Less from Each Other* (New York: Basic Books, 2011), especially Part II, "Networked: In Intimacy, New Solitudes," 151–305.

[56] The dangers of the opposite trend are alluded to in Ward and Himes, "'Growing Apart': The Rise of Inequality," 122.

Grace at the End of Life

to health care disparities in those instances where a global accountability represents too ambitious a goal. Of course, this concern reflects the need to inculcate solidarity as a more regular part of the moral life through the kinds of practices just detailed, but, in the interim, making this kind of accommodation is perfectly reasonable given that so much remains to be done to promote solidarity more effectively.

Beyond the narrow sense of autonomy that necessitates greater training in solidarity, there is also a second, institutional form of inertia standing in the way of a more globally-conscious approach to end-of-life care, this one lodged in the structures of Catholic health care itself. This is quite significant because, as a key provider of care, especially long-term care, Catholic health care creates a key institutional context within which many of the end-of-life decisions envisioned here occur. Yet Catholic health care is not always structured to promote a twofold discernment process that examines both local and global realities. Consider again the case of a patient in a persistent vegetative state who has chosen, after the twofold discernment process outlined above, to issue an advance directive requesting the discontinuation of artificial nutrition and hydration after this diagnosis has become effectively irreversible. Unfortunately, the structures of a Catholic hospital could end up preventing a patient's care team from honoring precisely this kind of request, for at least two reasons.

First, although health care teams are committed to honoring the autonomy of their patients, a certain kind of institutional inertia can complicate the decision-making process, especially with incapacitated patients, like those in a persistent vegetative state. For a variety of reasons, including fear of litigation, health care teams often cede power to surrogates in these situations, but the surrogate decision-maker is not always held accountable to the patient's wishes, even when those wishes have been expressed in an advance directive. As a result, physicians have observed that advance directives "have been disappointingly ineffective...because of barriers that are conceptual (general reluctance to explore death and dying), structural (inadequate clinical training, etc.) and procedural (restrictions on who can serve as a health care agent or proxy)."[57] Some of this can be addressed by encouraging patients to develop advanced planning for end-of-life decisions in a process that emphasizes more than just advance directives, but a complete solution must attend to the fact that there is "an organizational and professional failure to empower clinicians to support the patient's documented moral discernment" even in Catholic hospitals.[58]

---

[57] Angelo E. Volandes and Aretha Delight Davis, "Advance Care Planning Leads to Wished-For Care," *Health Progress* 98, no. 6 (2017), 43.
[58] Volandes and Davis, "Advance Care Planning Leads to Wished-For Care"; quote from Rachelle Barina, email to author, September 30, 2018.

Second, another structural issue stems from a combination of the ERDs' approach to advance directives and the developing tradition on artificial nutrition and hydration for patients in a persistent vegetative state. Directive 24 indicates that a Catholic health care institution "will not honor an advance directive that is contrary to Catholic teaching." Similarly, Directive 59 proclaims, "The free and informed judgment made by a competent adult patient [and by extension a legally designated proxy] concerning the use or withdrawal of life-sustaining procedures should always be respected and morally complied with, unless it is contrary to Catholic moral teaching." When this guidance is coupled with John Paul II's papal allocution and the CDF's clarification of that speech, the result is an ambiguity surrounding advance directives requesting the cessation of artificial nutrition and hydration when one is diagnosed in a persistent vegetative state.[59] In fact, when the United States bishops revised Directive 58 in 2009 to account for the magisterial developments concerning patients in a persistent vegetative state, Ron Hamel and Thomas Nairn provided guidance about the revisions for people working in Catholic health care ministry and explicitly acknowledged that "there may be the occasional situation, such as some patients in a persistent vegetative state, when what the patient is requesting through his or her advance directive is not consistent with the moral teachings of the Church. In these few cases, the Catholic health care facility would not be able to comply."[60] Now, in practice, Catholic health care facilities are not routinely intervening to object to a patient's advance directives, even in cases like this, out of a respect for the consciences and discernment processes of patients and their families. Nevertheless, the fact remains that the language of the ERDs at least creates an ambiguity on this matter, meaning that if the proverbial winds were to change, the structures would be in place to undermine a patient who employed the twofold discernment process in this situation. Consequently, it would be helpful to clarify this issue so that patients might, in good conscience, accept their invitation to cooperate with grace at the end of life in the way that befits their situation before God.

CONCLUSION

The two obstacles just described illustrate that getting the faithful to adopt a twofold discernment process for end-of-life care will likely be an uphill battle, especially in the United States. The Catholic community ought to commit itself to this battle, however, because so much

---

[59] Hamel, "The CDF Document," 6.
[60] Ron Hamel and Thomas Nairn, "The New Directive 58: What Does It Mean?" *Health Progress* 91, no. 1 (2010): 70–72.

is at stake. The twofold process of discerning ordinary and extraordinary means in both a local and a global context has a real potential to combat some of the most dangerous tendencies of the recent ballooning of ordinary means. Moreover, this approach reflects the best of the Catholic Church's long commitment to a transformative concern for the poor, and it suggests a way that Catholic health care ethics might embrace Pope Francis's vision for a "Church which is poor and for the poor."[61] Just as importantly, a twofold discernment process promotes a greater openness to grace, counteracting the recent tendency to preemptively restrict grace at the end of life. The road to making this global approach to end-of-life care a reality may be challenging, and it may be fraught with the frictions of sin both personal and structural, but insofar as this approach springs from the conviction that grace is at work in the world, it has every reason to hope that grace will be provided for all the steps along the way. **M**

---

[61] Pope Francis, "Address to Representatives of the Communications Media," March 16, 2013, w2.vatican.va/content/francesco/en/speeches/2013/march/documents/papa-francesco_20130316_rappresentanti-media.html.

A Voice in the Wilderness: Reimagining the Role of a Catholic Health Care Mission Leader

Michael McCarthy

"WE FIRED OVER 300 patients last year." Firing patients is not a common practice in health care; moreover, it is a less common practice for mission leaders to tout their firing. When pressed on why they were fired, he said that they often failed to show up to appointments, were not compliant with their medication, and "We were wasting a lot of resources and time supporting them." This particular group of patients, he said, simply did not understand how "disruptive" it was to not to show up to their appointments. While it may be true that these patients were "disruptive," I pressed him on who these patients were and if there were reasons that they may not have been able to make their appointments. He noted that many of these patients were Medicare patients with significant commutes, but "we have difficulty getting reimbursed for them anyway…." I later recounted this story and expressed shock—perhaps naïvely—that a mission leader would promote or advocate for firing a group of patients who by all estimations constituted a vulnerable patient population.

This story demonstrates two realities of the role of mission leaders. First, they are privy and can shape the inner workings and challenges of a health system. Second, they often oversee spiritual care and ethics departments and are often called on to navigate moral questions in Catholic health care that arise at the beginning and end of life. Their involvement at the executive level makes them acutely aware of the financial reality of health care, while their role in spiritual care and ethics can make them aware of the social challenges faced by many patients, families, and hospital staff. Thus, the mission leader finds herself in a unique place at board meetings. How does one speak to the economic focus that shapes the imagination of many health care executives, while remaining rooted in a theological voice that may resonate like one crying out in the wilderness, speaking against decisions that diminish the social ministry of Catholic health care but may benefit its financial margin?

In short, one aspect of the mission leader's role is to serve as a prophetic voice capable of drawing on her theological background to

A Voice in the Wilderness 115

more deeply articulate the mission of continuing Jesus's healing ministry, as it is often referred to in Catholic health care. Yet one of the factors that might contribute to the hesitancy of theologians pursuing the role of a mission leader emerges out of the perception that the role addresses only a narrow subset of ethical questions around contraception, sterilization, abortion, and increasingly complex questions around cooperation in health system mergers.[1] However, a major role of the theologian as mission leader is to be critical of that which is antithetical to the mission of Catholic health care. While this is inclusive of procedures prohibited in Catholic hospitals, it also includes ways of addressing socially unjust structures that limit patient access or promote health inequalities both in the hospital and in the community.

The first part of this essay describes the evolution of the role of mission leadership within Catholic health care and draws on data generated from a Catholic Health Association (CHA) survey to describe why more theologians would benefit Catholic health care. While theologians may fit the need described by CHA, the second section argues that the narrow subset of issues addressed typically within the Catholic bioethics literature limits the number of theologians who may otherwise consider serving in mission leadership roles. Nevertheless, the ERDs emphasis on questions of social ethics needs further theological reflection. Increasing theological voices focused on social inequalities within Catholic health care will augment the scope of issues addressed in Catholic bioethics. Third, the essay considers the vocation of a theologian and whether the understanding of that vocation fits with the context of a health care mission leader. In an effort to assess whether a theologian's understanding of her role fits with the needs of a mission leader, this section explores how the mission role would benefit from a more explicitly theological foundation. With a firmer theological foundation for mission leaders, the essay concludes by arguing that there are a range of concerns found within Catholic health care which would benefit from analysis by theologically trained mission leaders. However, Catholic health care needs to create an academic space for teaching and research while serving as a mission leader. Theologians present an opportunity for Catholic health care to utilize the role of the mission leaders to analyze the moral challenges facing health care in the US, expand the range of social ethics questions addressed, and better speak to the mission and identity of Catholic health care.

---

[1] United States Conference of Catholic Bishops, "Ethical and Religious Directives for Health Care Services, Sixth Edition," www.usccb.org/about/doctrine/ethical-and-religious-directives/upload/ethical-religious-directives-catholic-health-service-sixth-edition-2016-06.pdf.

TWO PIPELINE PROBLEMS

There are many opportunities for people trained in theology to work within Catholic health care, but there are relatively few PhD trained theologians pursuing a career in health care. More perplexing, these opportunities exist alongside the well-documented challenges for PhDs in obtaining tenure-track jobs. An article in *The Atlantic* details that over 45 percent of PhD graduates have been unable to find employment either in academia or an industry-related field post-graduation.[2] The American Academy of Religion job advertisement data for 2016-2017 reveals an 8.6 percent decrease in faculty positions but notes a slight 4 percent increase in non-faculty position offerings at colleges and universities.[3] While tenure-track jobs remain particularly scarce, Catholic health care has a steady stream of available of jobs in mission leadership.

However, few theologians have pursued these posts as viable postdoctoral options despite the historical influence theologians have had in creating important discourses within bioethics. As Jonsen describes, moral theologians "gave an exposition of the fundamental moral principles derived from natural law and divine revelation, followed by casuistic analysis of specific topics, invariably including abortion, contraception, sterilization, euthanasia, and various types of surgery...."[4] These foundational issues laid the groundwork for the medical ethics questions that formed the bedrock of the Ethical and Religious Directives (ERDs) since their first writing in 1949.[5] These theologians, however, worked outside of the hospital setting. The "medico-moral" issues, as they were termed, were addressed in practice by the women religious involved in the day to day operations of the hospital in executive administration positions. However, as the number of religious declined, lay leaders—often lacking any theological formation—began to fill these roles.

The role of lay leaders in Catholic health care emerged amidst another transition from individual hospitals, sponsored as works of religious sisters, to larger health systems owned by corporations led by lay leaders. The catalyst for these changes was dictated by US policies

---

[2] Laura McKenna, "The Ever-Tightening Job Market for Phds: Why Do So Many People Continue to Pursue Doctorates?" *The Atlantic,* April 21, 2016, www.theatlantic.com/education/archive/2016/04/bad-job-market-phds/479205/.
[3] American Academy of Religion, "Job Advertisement Data 2016-2017 American Academy of Religion and Society of Biblical Literature," www.aarweb.org/sites/default/files/pdfs/Career_Services/2016-2017%20jobs_report_1617.pdf
[4] Albert R. Jonsen, *The Birth of Bioethics* (New York: Oxford University Press, 1998), 36.
[5] Kevin O'Rourke, Thomas Kopfensteiner, and Ronald Hamel, "A Brief History: A Summary of the Development of the Ethical and Religious Directives for Catholic Health Care Services," *Health Progress* 82, no. 6 (2001): 18.

that affected the economics of health care related to Medicare, Medicaid, and an increasingly complex insurance and reimbursement structure. The shift to third-party payers "encouraged hospitals to respond to the market incentives of increased demand by providing more expensive and better care, in areas that were most likely to be reimbursed."[6] Beginning in the 1960s, Catholic hospitals gradually became a part of health systems competing in an emerging health care market.

The sixties marked a significant time of change in the life of Catholic health care. "Between 1965 and 1975 the number of Catholic hospitals dropped from 803 to 671, and the number of sisters involved in health care fell from 13,618 to 8,980."[7] While the number of hospitals themselves has remained relatively unchanged, with 654 Catholic hospitals operating in the US still today, waves of hospital mergers have connected these once independent hospitals into a network of larger and more complex health systems.[8] The shift in the health care landscape, coupled with the decline in religious sisters working in health care, resulted in nearly all hospital CEOs being run by lay leadership.[9] The rise in lay leadership at the upper echelons of Catholic health care created initial space for women religious to serve as the first generation of mission leaders at these institutions. These roles focused on having an understanding of Catholic spiritual tradition—pastoral care, chaplains, creating and nurturing the faith of a religious work—and monitoring the "medico-moral" questions that would arise in the context of the ERDs. However, as the number of women religious continued to decline there was a need and interest in creating and maintaining positions focused on the Catholic identity of these institutions via ethics and, more recently, through the role of mission leaders.

A 2013 survey conducted by the Catholic Health Association describes mission leaders in Catholic health systems.[10] Mission leaders are most likely to be religious sisters or lay women, slightly outnumbering lay men. The majority of these respondents (62 percent) were between ages 55-65. Among current mission leaders, 16 percent possess a doctoral degree and 74 percent hold a master's degree; the area of study for most of these degrees (68%) is theology or spirituality.

---

[6] Christopher J. Kauffman, *Ministry and Meaning: A Religious History of Catholic Health Care in the United States* (New York: Crossroad, 1995), 277.
[7] Kauffman, *Ministry and Meaning*, 283.
[8] Catholic Health Association, "U.S. Catholic Health Care: 2018," www.chausa.org/docs/default-source/default-document-library/cha_2018_miniprofile7aa087f4dff26ff58685ff00005b1bf3.pdf?sfvrsn=2.
[9] Emily Trancik and Rachelle Barina, "What Makes a Catholic Hospital Catholic," *U.S. Catholic*, March 25, 2015, www.uscatholic.org/articles/201503/what-makes-catholic-hospital-catholic-29861.
[10] Brian P. Smith and Sr. Patricia Talone, RSM, "New Survey: Mission Leaders Respond Executive Summary of the 2013 CHA Mission Leader Survey," *Health Progress* 94, no. 6 (2013): 70-75.

Additionally, the survey asked the participants to identify educational areas that they thought would be most beneficial for future mission leaders. Those working as mission leaders identified their ideal replacements to be people grounded in theology and ethics who possess pastoral sensibilities.[11] While this profile may not apply to every theologian in training, it does fit the profile of many theologians who may not currently see health care as a viable avenue for a theologian to consider. This perception is due in large part to the narrow scope of issues addressed historically in Catholic bioethics, mostly by those not working directly within the lived reality of Catholic health care.

OBSTACLES AND OPPORTUNITIES FOR THEOLOGIANS IN MISSION LEADERSHIP

A literature review conducted on Catholic bioethics between 1980 and 2017 generates a narrow set of issues concentrated on beginning and end of life questions.[12] The review found that nearly 85% of the published books and essays focused on a small set of issues: "the beginning of life (procreation/contraception, reproductive technologies, marriage, abortion), the end of life (withholding and withdrawing treatment, MANH, PVS, euthanasia, physician-assisted suicide, futility, pain management), organ donation, research with human subjects, stem cells, culture wars, conscience, and genetics."[13] While these issues are important, and occupy a central concern in the eyes of many local bishops, they do not represent the entirety of bioethical questions that warrant critical theological engagement. Rather, the collection of issues represents a particular understanding of bioethics and an interpretation of moral theology rooted in the neo-Thomistic and manualist tradition. While this framework has served as foundational to the "medico-moral" questions in the nascent stages of bioethics, the social ethics questions facing health care today remain overlooked.

Over the last three and a half decades, an average of two publications per year addressed bioethical questions that engaged questions of social ethics and Catholic social teaching. These essays and books focused on questions in global bioethics, human rights, social justice and participation, or explored bioethical questions from a liberationist

---

[11] Smith and Talone, "New Survey," 72-73: "The respondents indicated that spirituality (71%), ministry (66%), theology (65%), and ethics (64%) would be the most beneficial areas."
[12] M. Therese Lysaught and Michael McCarthy, "A Social Praxis for US Health Care: Revisioning Catholic Bioethics Via Catholic Social Thought," *Journal for the Society of Christian Ethics* 38, no. 2 (2018): 111-130.
[13] Lysaught and McCarthy, "A Social Praxis for US Health Care," 113.

A Voice in the Wilderness 119

perspective.[14] Despite the innovation within these publications, they remain few and far between. More of these publications are needed given the social ethical questions facing health care today; however, these concerns have historically fallen outside of the purview of Catholic bioethics.

To broaden these theological issues for mission leaders, one could turn to the ERDs. The ERDs are a collaborative resource developed by theologians, health care professionals, and the United States Conference of Catholic Bishops and provide guidelines for practices, procedures, and policies at Catholic hospitals. They are divided into six parts, each part composed of directives that establish normative expectations within Catholic healthcare. Part I describes the social responsibilities of Catholic health care, while Part II establishes the pastoral, spiritual, and sacramental care for those within the hospital. Part III focuses on the importance of the patient physician relationship, emphasizing the importance of honesty, trust, and conscience. Parts IV and V of the ERDs are perhaps most familiar. Part IV focuses on questions at the beginning of life (contraception, reproduction, obstetrical complications), while Part V provides guidelines for understanding Catholic norms for clinical care at the end of life. Finally, Part VI of the directives, the subject of much discussion and recent revision in the sixth edition, establishes a framework through which hospitals and health systems can discern various aspects of collaboration with non-Catholic partners. Despite the breadth of the directives, the emphasis within Catholic health care centers on the clinical and individual aspects of Parts IV and V.

Part IV provides the familiar phrasing that prohibits the use of contraceptives to prevent pregnancy, direct abortions, and the use of assisted reproductive technologies that result in procreation outside of the marital act. While this list of prohibitions may seem easily understood, this section raises important theological questions around understanding the nature of the moral act, the principle of double effect, and the intentions of moral agents. Alongside these more well-trodden theological questions, placed more subtly in the introduction, are questions of justice raised with respect to exploring the ways in which the Church can collaborate to "alleviate the causes of the high infant mortality rate and to provide adequate health care to mothers and their children before and after birth."[15] While not explicitly addressing this fact, it is important to note that the US infant mortality rate is highest

---

[14] Only 75 publications came out during 1980-2017 that focused specifically on questions of social justice and Catholic bioethics. The topics most frequently raised pertained to access to health care and HIV/AIDS, with occasional attention to end-of-life issues, reproductive issues, genetics, global poverty, and recently *Laudato Si'*. See Lysaught and McCarthy, "A Social Praxis for US Health Care," 114.

[15] USCCB, *Ethical and Religious Directives*, Part IV, introduction.

amongst black infants at 11.2 per 1000 live births. Comparatively, white infants have a mortality rate less than half of that, at 5 per 1000.[16] These statistics warrant not only a focus on increasing access to prenatal care but also ensuring that there is a safe environment in which children have the opportunity to develop and flourish. While what is often emphasized in this part of the directives are the prohibited clinical functions, the directives are concerned not just with the delivery of health care but with questions of justice that affect the health of vulnerable populations. While mission leaders should understand distinctive prohibitions in Catholic health care, they should be concerned and able to speak equally to the social injustices in the communities within which Catholic health care exists.[17]

Unlike Part IV, Part V offers only one prohibition, not directly ending the life of a patient (Directive 60). Most of the directives in this section center on the importance of establishing extraordinary and ordinary treatments at the end of life and ensuring that those are understood from the perspective of the patient (Directive, 56-59). While much theological dispute has arisen out of the addition of directive 58 on artificial nutrition and hydration, few theological debates counter the technologizing of the dying process and the financial challenges and racial inequalities that emerge at the end of life.[18] Furthermore, a nuanced understanding of death, suffering, and accompaniment would benefit from further theological exploration and practical implementation.[19] When these topics do surface, they typically occur in an academic classroom or scholarly contribution—like this one—and fail to form or transform the way in which care at the end of life is delivered in clinical practice. More theologians in hospitals, health care systems, or medical schools witnessing and reflecting on these realities could broaden the theological factors constituent to the practice of health care.

---

[16] Imari Smith, Keisha L. Bentley-Edwards, Salimah El-Amin and William Darity, Jr., "Eradicating Black Infant Mortality," socialequity.duke.edu/sites/socialequity.duke.edu/files/site-images/EradicatingBlackInfantMortality-March2018%20FINAL.pdf.
[17] Michael Rozier, "Religion and Public Health: Moral Tradition as Both Problem and Solution," *Journal of Religion and Health* 56, no. 3 (2017): 1052-1063.
[18] Richard Payne, "Racially Associated Disparities in Hospice and Palliative Care Access: Acknowledging the Facts While Addressing the Opportunities to Improve," *Journal of Palliative Medicine* 19, no. 2 (2016): 131-133.
[19] Jeffrey P. Bishop, *The Anticipatory Corpse: Medicine, Power, and the Care of the Dying* (Notre Dame: University of Notre Dame Press, 2011); Richard Payne, Gwendolyn London, Sharon R. Latson, "Key Topics on End of Life Care for African Americans," *Duke Institute on Care at the End of Life*, divinity.duke.edu/sites/divinity.duke.edu/files/documents/tmc/KTFULL.pdf.

A Voice in the Wilderness 121

While Parts IV and V beg for further theological and social ethical reflections, Part I explicitly situates social ethics and social responsibility as the normative foundations for the mission of Catholic health care institutions. The introduction to Part I of the directives emphasizes key themes in Catholic social teaching that require the attention of hospitals. Catholic health care ministries should be mindful of human dignity as the foundation of their work and the praxis of the preferential option for the poor in the way it cares for "the particular health needs of the underinsured and uninsured" (ERD, Introduction, Part I). Yet the responsibility of Catholic health care goes beyond the clinical aspect to participate in the common good by optimizing "economic, political, and social conditions" that support the fulfillment of "fundamental rights of all individuals" (ERD, Introduction, Part I). Directive Three states:

> In accord with its mission, Catholic health care should distinguish itself by service to and advocacy for those people whose social condition puts them at the margins of our society and makes them particularly vulnerable to discrimination: the poor; the uninsured and the underinsured; children and the unborn; single parents; the elderly; those with incurable diseases and chemical dependencies; racial minorities; immigrants and refugees. In particular, the person with mental or physical disabilities, regardless of the cause or severity, must be treated as a unique person of incomparable worth, with the same right to life and to adequate health care as all other persons.

While the list is expansive, the need to care for members of the LBGTQ community, particularly the health needs of gender non-conforming persons, should be added.[20] This addition, however, only emphasizes the depth of the challenges in living up to the social responsibility of Catholic health care. There exists ample theological justification for including social questions as foundational to the mission of Catholic health care.

However, these concerns are often limited by the context of Catholic healthcare that, as our narrative from the beginning illustrated, is in the midst of a competitive and economically driven health care environment. There are significant financial challenges to living up to the social responsibility of Catholic health care given the current structure of the US health care system that, at least for now, remains based predominately on a "fee-for-service" model. This model of health care

---

[20] David Albert Jones, "Gender Reassignment Surgery: A Catholic Bioethical Analysis," *Theological Studies* 79, no. 2 (2018): 314-338. See also Michael McCarthy, "Bewildering Accompaniment: The Ethics of Caring for Gender Non-Conforming Children and Adolescents," in *Catholic Bioethics and Social Justice: The Praxis of US Health Care in a Globalized World,* ed. M. Therese Lysaught and Michael McCarthy (Collegeville: Liturgical Press, 2018), 113-127.

relies both on a solid mission base and a healthy financial margin. Financial concerns are relevant to furthering of the mission of Catholic health care; yet these economic realities cannot be the primary hermeneutic for mission leaders. When the theological voice joins the chorus of those whose chief concern is the financial health of the institution, the mission of the health system itself is in trouble. John Mudd, a retired senior vice-president for mission at Providence-St. Joseph, speaks from his own experience when saying:

> Those of us who have lived most of our lives in the world of secular business are comfortable talking about financial and operational performance. We gravitate to those issues, and they tend to occupy our focus. But ask us to assess the mission effectiveness of our ministries or the quality of our spiritual care arguably the distinguishing characteristics of these Catholic institutions and many of us become tongue-tied.[21]

There are many mission leaders who transition to the role from areas such as finance, social work, and nursing. While those transitions are greatly needed, so too are theologians who, as part of their vocation, can articulate the depth of the social mission of Catholic health care working in a health care context.

A THEOLOGICAL VOCATION: REMEMBERING THE HEALING MINISTRY OF JESUS CHRIST

The magisterial description of the theologian's vocation, articulated only within the last thirty years, focuses primarily on questions of authority. *Donum Veritatis* emphasizes the role of faith, seeking "Truth" which is "the living God and [God's] plan for Salvation revealed in Jesus Christ" (no. 8). In this quest for truth, the document emphasizes that theologians should rely on philosophy and human sciences (no. 10). Nevertheless, "When the Magisterium proposes 'in a definitive way' truths concerning faith and morals, which, even if not divinely revealed, are nevertheless strictly and intimately connected with Revelation, these must be firmly accepted and held" (no. 22). This top down description of a theological vocation has been challenged by theologians themselves because it seems to restrict rather than welcome dialogue.[22] Yet the theological vocation as described in

---

[21] John O. Mudd, "From CEO to Mission Leader," *America*, July 18, 2005, www.americamagazine.org/issue/537/article/ceo-mission-leader.

[22] See Richard McCormick, *The Critical Calling: Reflections on Moral Dilemmas Since Vatican II* (Washington, DC: Georgetown University Press, 2006), 71-94. McCormick recounts an exchange around the Magisterial prohibition of direct sterilization in 1980 that led to a series of correspondences with then Archbishop Jerome Hamer. McCormick challenged the theological argument used in constructing the

Donum Veritatis is the framework that has been followed by mission leaders in Catholic health care.[23] Even under this framework, there are only a few issues that have been spoken of "in a definitive way" and they only cover a small subset of very specific issues related to contraception and the direct and voluntary killing of innocent life such as in an abortion and acts of euthanasia.[24]

Even within this restricted framework, there is much theology and education to be done with clinical staff about what constitutes a direct versus indirect abortion in the context of an emergency such as the one that presented in St. Joseph's hospital in Phoenix, AZ, or the more recent controversies surrounding United Kingdom's legal decision to withdraw treatment from two infants over the wishes of their parents.[25] Thus, even following the ecclesial definition, there are important points of theological nuance that require careful thought by theologians before difficult decisions are made, not after. This model of theology as a reaction needs to be reconsidered in light of the implementation of Vatican II in which theologians "fulfill their vocation by participating as advisors and trusted collaborators."[26]

Theological definitions of vocation, and the specific vocation of the theologian, highlight the importance of the place from which one does theology and recognizes the challenges of living out that vocation. Edward Hahnenberg posits, a "[v]ocation brings to the surface a deep and dynamic tension within the Christian life, namely, the tension between comfort offered in the gospel message and its unrelenting challenge."[27] The challenge of living out a theological vocation amid the health care landscape is presented in the tensions between a service-oriented profession, the economic reality of health care, and the immense need of patients within health care ministries. On an individual level, theological voices can help frame the suffering and interruptions that occur daily in the midst of an individual's illness and

---

document. He concluded his multi-letter exchange with the Archbishop by noting, "The critical aspect of theological response to Roman interventions is an inseparable part of doctrinal purification and is an absolutely indispensable aspect of a theologian's loyalty to the Holy See" (77).

[23] Bradford E. Hinze, *Prophetic Obedience: Ecclesiology for a Dialogical Church* (Maryknoll: Orbis Books, 2016).

[24] Richard R. Gaillardetz, "The Ordinary Universal Magisterium: Unresolved Questions," *Theological Studies* 63, no.3 (2002): 452.

[25] John J. Paris, Michael P. Moreland, and Brian M. Cummings, "The Catholic Tradition on the Due Use of Medical Remedies: The Charlie Gard Case," *Theological Studies* 79, no. 1 (2018): 165-181. Kevin O'Rourke, "Complications: A Catholic Hospital, a Pregnant Mother and a Questionable Excommunication," *America*, August 2, 2010, www.americamagazine.org/issue/744/article/complications.

[26] Bradford E. Hinze, "A Decade of Disciplining Theologians," *Horizons*, 37, no. 1 (2010): 126.

[27] Edward P. Hahnenberg, *Awakening Vocation: A Theology of Christian Call* (Collegeville: Liturgical Press, 2010): 195.

"[w]ith the whole people of God...to adhere to the faith to penetrate it more deeply through right judgment, and to apply it more fully in daily life...."[28] The role of the theologian in mission leadership can point to God's presence in the reality both inside and outside of the hospital walls. The theologian, moreover, can name injustices and so draw the health care system to pay particular attention to the unmet needs of the communities in which they reside. Shawn Copeland offers a significant insight when she notes that theologians "do theology because we want to collaborate fundamentally in bringing about a different kind of world in the here-and-now."[29] The need for mission leadership in Catholic health care represents an opportunity for theologians to more seriously articulate in writing and in the boardrooms the real social challenges and cost of continuing the healing ministry of Jesus Christ in today's world.

THE SOCIO-ETHICAL DIMENSION OF MISSION LEADERSHIP

The multi-dimensional role of the mission leader raises questions that challenge institutions to reach beyond the ever-present fiscal challenges and wrestle with more difficult questions that speak to the social dimension of practicing Catholic health care. While the literature on the intersection of social ethics, Catholic social teaching, and bioethics is scant, their interconnectivity is real. Questions of social justice play out in the organizational questions of compensation and community outreach. Within the community, the acute clinical and public health needs become apparent more readily and are often tied to race and gender. Likewise, there is increased awareness about the way in which health systems care for and are attentive to the environmental impact of Catholic health care. When considering each of these various aspects of the lived reality, the mission leader plays a vital role in not only identifying social inequalities but pushing others within the leadership team of the health system to explore solutions to complex problems befitting of the social responsibilities of Catholic health care that reflect its social mission.

In 2009, the USCCB collaborated with labor officials and Catholic Health Association president Sr. Carol Keehan to develop a document

---

[28] Mary Ann Donovan, "The Vocation of the Theologian," *Theological Studies* 65, no. 1 (2004): 9.
[29] M. Shawn Copeland, "Racism and the Vocation of the Theologian," *Spiritus: A Journal of Christian Spirituality*, Vol. 2, no. 1 (2002): 26.

offering guidance to both health care leadership and workers to determine how best to create a just work environment.[30] Like Catholic universities, Catholic health care has also been forced to reconcile a tradition that supports the role of unions and workers' rights in their teachings but has opposed them in their institutions.[31] Two issues highlight the need for mission leaders to be attentive to workers' rights in Catholic health care: just wages and their participation in the care economy. Mission leaders have an important role to play not just in articulating the theological position that supports unions but to raise questions around just wages, ensuring that all members of the community are able to participate in the community, from environmental services to the executive leadership. As a mission leader, one may have to raise difficult questions during financial crises when it is tempting to sacrifice the lowest wage workers. A theological voice that aligns with those on the margins needs to be aware of social challenges the lowest wage workers may face given the prospect of job loss. They might offer a proposal that shifts the financial burden to the executive or argues for other cost-saving measures, rather than relying on those responsible for creating a safe and sanitary work environment. More importantly, with respect to unions, it is fundamental that open lines of communication be maintained, and that fair and transparent negotiation processes are established. While finances do have a role to play, it is the Catholic mission that frames the financial argument, not the other way around.

A second feature worthy of consideration is the way in which Catholic health care participates in and influences the care economy, dominated mostly by women of color. Referencing research conducted by Glenn and Folbre, Christine Firer Hinze notes that "studies worldwide confirm three striking facts: the care economy's (paid or unpaid) primary agents are women; markets and civil society depend upon a functioning care economy; and markets and civil society tend to underacknowledge and undervalue, and therefore exploit, caring labor."[32] Working with uninsured and underinsured populations makes the reliance on family care agents (paid or unpaid) essential. It is important that the health care staff are made aware of the challenges that families may be facing, ensuring that sufficient resources are available. While

---

[30] The US Conference of Catholic Bishops affirmed the right to unionize at Catholic hospitals in "Respecting the Just Rights of Workers: Guidance and Options for Catholic Health Care and Unions," www.usccb.org/issues-and-action/ human-life-and-dignity/labor-employment/.

[31] Daniel P. Dwyer, "Unions in Catholic Health Care: A Paradox," in *Catholic Bioethics and Social Justice: The Praxis of US Healthcare in a Globalized World*, ed. M. Therese Lysaught and Michael McCarthy (Collegeville: Liturgical Press, 2018), 165-177.

[32] Christine Firer Hinze, "Catholic Social Thought and Work Justice," *Theological Studies* 70, no. 1 (2016): 212-213.

these resources would certainly include spiritual and pastoral support, they may also include financial support to defer costs and enable a safe transition of care to a different facility or home. Many of these conversations are already ongoing, and social workers are aware of the strain of caring for a loved one outside of the hospital. Nevertheless, there has been little theological or ethical engagement on the reliance of Catholic health care on the care economy.[33] These topics concern a wide range of hospital personnel from the highest paid executive to the least paid environmental service worker. This range only heightens the importance of having a theological voice capable of reflecting on the mission-based significance of just wages. In addition to organizational concerns, mission leaders need to be cognizant also of the social challenges facing the communities in which the organization operates.

One of the recent and poignant public-health issues is the question of gun violence, which has reached epidemic proportion in the U.S. On one level, gun violence can be considered a critical care issue—victims arrive to be cared for in the emergency department and in trauma units.[34] On another level, gun violence raises important questions around mission, particularly about how a Catholic health system ought to respond to this public health crisis that disproportionately affects black communities. Nicholas Kristof proposes a public-health strategy to reduce the number of guns and those who have access to them via a series of legislative moves.[35] He bases his plan in the safety successes produced through the regulation of automobiles throughout the latter half of the twentieth century, which resulted in decrease motor vehicle fatalities from 9 per 100 million in 1946 to 1 per 100 million in 2016. Enacting laws requires comprehensive advocacy and multi-sector partnerships.

Cardinal Blaise Cupich partnered with Loyola University Health System, a member of Trinity Health, to advocate for Illinois state legislation to require licensing of gun dealers. He sought Loyola out to work with members of the Emergency Department and Spiritual Care and Education Department to emphasize the importance of advocacy efforts for and with vulnerable populations as constitutive of the identity of Catholic health care institutions. Advocacy for legislation, however, is one piece. The Spiritual Care and Education Department also

---

[33] Sandra Sullivan-Dunbar, *Human Dependency and Christian Ethics* (Cambridge: Cambridge University Press, 2017).
[34] Michelle Byrne, Virginia McCarthy, Abigail Silva, and Sharon Homan, "Healthcare Providers on the Frontline: Responding to the Gun Violence Epidemic," in *Catholic Bioethics and Social Justice: The Praxis of US Healthcare in a Globalized World*, ed. M. Therese Lysaught and Michael McCarthy (Collegeville: Liturgical Press, 2018), 31-45.
[35] Nicholas Kristof, "How to Reduce Shootings," *New York Times*, May 18, 2018, www.nytimes.com/interactive/2017/11/06/opinion/how-to-reduce-shootings.html.

initiated collaborations with local congregations on gun violence strategies rooted in reconciliation, forgiveness, and family support in the hospital. The work of the Cardinal and hospital staff sends a message with theological undertones that speak to the importance of advocacy and collaboration to create a safe environment in which the community lives, works, and plays.

Engagement with the local community also requires socio-ethical analysis of what causes particular communities to have more violence, lower life expectancies, and increased health disparities. For many of these communities, race plays a significant factor. Shawn Copeland challenges theologians to recognize as integral to their vocation an attentiveness to the social sin of racism. She argues, "Our theology must repudiate the principalities and powers of society and resist their efforts to seduce its spirit-filled, prophetic, critical, and creative impulse. In the twilight of American culture, telling the truth about white racist supremacy is a theological obligation, no matter how cauterizing those truths may be."[36] These racial inequalities are present each day in the health system and their realities affect patients, communities, and those working in health care systems. Theologians willing to take up Copeland's challenge can lend their voices to considering race as a foundational question of mission leadership in Catholic health care.

Additionally, racial divides are of increased interest as concerns about migration rise in urgency and importance within the social justice agenda of Catholic health care. Kuczewski, Medina, and Blair have proposed that clinics implement a guide to inform health care staff of some cues to support undocumented patients and their families.[37] They argue that it is paramount to ensure that hospitals and clinics are safe places and that their patients' immigration status will not be shared with immigration services. While the issue of immigration has reached a political fever pitch, it is clear among health care professional organizations and the leadership of many Catholic health care systems, Trinity Health in particular, that DACA physicians and medical students are not only welcomed into the work force but can and do play a vital role in caring for immigrant and refugee communities. To have a theological voice that can speak to the significance of the historical commitment of the Catholic Church to immigrants and the scriptural roots of "welcoming the stranger" can lead to deeper insights and, hopefully, resources that can better position Catholic health care as allies with those communities maligned and pushed to the margins of society.

---

[36] Copeland, "Racism and the Vocation of the Theologian," 22.
[37] Mark Kuczewski, Johanna Medina, and Amy Blair, "Treating Fear: Sanctuary Doctoring," *Neiswanger Institute of Bioethics & Healthcare Leadership*, hsd.luc.edu/bioethics/content/sanctuary-doctor/.

Questions of worker rights, race, gun violence, and immigration are areas that are not only emerging in Catholic bioethics, they are still being formulated in secular bioethics. To have theologians participate in the shaping of social bioethics questions can hark back to the days in which theologians shaped bioethical discourse as the field itself was being formed. The social injustices that face individuals and communities will eventually present themselves as some form of illness, disease, or acute medical event, sooner or later. Theologians in mission leadership roles who can articulate the breadth and depth of the tradition can likewise push the boundaries of what is considered a mission-based issue and better participate in continuing to shape the identity of Catholic health care that is widely perceived to consist in a list of services Catholic hospitals are unable to provide.

CONCLUSION: HEALTH CARE AS *LOCUS THEOLOGICUS*
Catholic health care functions as a theological locus from which theologians can raise critical questions that, as Shawn Copeland says, can help them "collaborate fundamentally in bringing about a different kind of world in the here-and-now."[38] However, Catholic health care is going to have to create space for theologians to join their enterprise. Most Catholic mission leaders serve as members of the executive leadership team and may have little time for theological reflection, much less writing. Creating new positions is essential, but this must be done in a way which attracts the type of theological talent that exists in the post-doctoral world. "Internships" are not typically what a post-doc theologian is seeking. These jobs, however, can be crafted to include more of an academic profile of teaching (residents, nurses, executives), research on mission based issues (akin to the ones highlighted above), clinical case studies, and service (learning the ins and outs of the health care system on a daily basis).

While the traditional concerns of abortion, contraception, and decisions at the end of life will not go anywhere, there is ample room to expand the socio-theological purview of mission leaders that will benefit the scope of Catholic health care ministries. Integrating PhD trained theologians into mission leadership positions allows for individuals to critically assess and articulate the ways in which Catholic health care participate in the healing ministry of Jesus Christ through its commitment to serve those pushed to the margins. Catholic health care benefits from the ability of mission leaders educated in theology, ethics, and spirituality, to speak to the theological foundations of Catholic health care and the social inequalities present in it, and can work

---

[38] Copeland, "Racism and the Vocation of the Theologian," 26.

collaboratively to address complex challenges in a way that reflects the mission of Catholic health care ministries in a broken world. **M**

Theologians in Catholic Healthcare Ministries: Breaking Beyond the Bond to Ethics

Darren M. Henson

CATHOLIC HEALTHCARE IN THE UNITED STATES relies upon and benefits from the contributions of theology. Historically, ethics served as the default locus where theology and medicine intersected in Catholic healthcare ministries (CHMs). Yet, as CHMs face increasingly intricate challenges today, they seek theological expertise on an expanding spectrum of issues. Pairing theologians exclusively with ethics no longer suffices to address the contemporary needs in CHMs.

The first part of this essay reviews historical markers indicating how theologians aligned with ethics in their service to CHMs in the U.S. This association became most clear beginning in the early twentieth century as theologians opined on clinical ethics procedures emerging from advances in medicine. The role of the theologian evolved to include organizational ethics and analysis of cooperation with moral wrongdoing. By the mid and late twentieth century, substantial changes in U.S. healthcare delivery and financing prompted Catholic hospitals and systems to partner with outside organizations, many of which are other-than-Catholic.

The second part of the essay spotlights areas beyond ethics where CHMs need theological expertise. I argue that theologians in CHM must move beyond the historical paradigm of problem-analysis-answer created by its pairing with ethics. Rather, the role of the theologian serves as a bearer of the broader Catholic tradition across multiple areas of a healthcare ministry. While ethics remains an important domain, five additional areas call for the gifts and skills of the theologian.

First, I explain how theologians specializing in social ethics provide an essential body of work that CHMs ought to more fully integrate. Second, CHMs need theologians to guide organizational discernment processes, distinct from the analysis of cooperation with moral wrongdoing. Third, the emergence of formation within CHMs must include sound theological depth. Relatedly, the fourth area features how sponsors increasingly raise questions pertaining to ecclesiology, the nature of ministry, and missiology which call for theological expertise. Finally, the theologian serving in CHM needs partnerships and dialogue with other theologians. The theologians in the academy, in CHMs, and in the chancery need insights from one another to honor and reflect the concrete and complex realities CHMs face.

This work focuses on CHMs in the American context. The scope pertains to a theological response to scientific and technological advancements from the late nineteenth century to the present when medicine and its financial and organizational structures substantially changed. My own professional and social perspective draws from formal academic training, years of experience working in Catholic healthcare systems, teaching theology in an academic setting, and being an active parishioner.

THE THEOLOGIAN AND MEDICINE

For centuries Catholic theologians have engaged matters of life, death, and health. Developments flowing from the Enlightenment dramatically altered the questions considered by theology and other disciplines. By the late nineteenth century, modernity anchored itself firmly in medicine. Therapies advanced from vaccine discoveries. Devices multiplied with inventions like x-ray, and processes accelerated toward standardization and professional licensing. The American Medical Association, founded in 1897, led the way in these and similar efforts, including the development of a code of professional ethics.[1] Catholic hospitals responded to the professional and social changes with steadfast commitment to their ministries while welcoming willing physician partners. Catholic researchers like priest psychiatrist Thomas Verner Moore embraced emerging scientific possibilities from the perspective of his Catholic faith.[2] Fr. Charles Moulinier, S.J., responded to the need for a unified and standardized Catholic approach to medicine in this time, and he hosted the first Catholic Health Association gathering (CHA; previously 'Hospital' association) in 1915.[3] Questions surfaced from Catholic hospitals regarding the moral permissibility of new clinical procedures.

Catholic theologians used the tradition that preceded them to produce resources giving moral direction on clinical procedures. By 1947, U.S. and Canadian theologians and healthcare professionals, respond-

---

[1] For an insightful overview of how modernity influenced the evolution of the American healthcare system, see Paul Starr and the American Council of Learned Societies, *The Social Transformation of American Medicine* (New York: Basic Books, 1982).
[2] Benedict Neenan, *Thomas Verner Moore: Psychiatrist, Educator, and Monk* (New York: Paulist Press, 2000).
[3] For a most helpful overview of the historical transition in Catholic healthcare in the U.S., see Christopher J. Kauffman, *Ministry and Meaning: A Religious History of Catholic Health Care in the United States* (New York: Crossroad, 1995).

ing to the groundswell of standardization, created the document *Ethical and Religious Directives for Catholic Hospitals* (ERDs).[4] Gerald Kelly, S.J., worked with the CHA on a second revision in 1956. Within a few years, he authored *Medico-Moral Problems*. The majority of issues addressed in these publications pertained to matters of human reproduction, pregnancy, and fertility.[5] This focus is unsurprising as Kelly's theology recycled the methodology of the moral manuals. Kelly and his Jesuit confrere, John C. Ford, S.J., maintained close alignment with papal teachings and magisterial writings.[6] Not only did theologians opine on matters of the rapidly emerging technologies and new procedures advanced by the scientific revolution, but even the popes of this era entered into the discourse in the neo-manualist vein,[7] perhaps none more so than Paul VI's 1968 encyclical *Humanae Vitae*.[8] Theological discourse following the encyclical's release reflected other methodologies in moral theology that germinated in the twentieth century, yet the manualist imagination like that of Ford and Kelly infiltrated most deeply into the policies and operations of CHMs. While alternative methodologies came from academia, the legacy of a manualist imagination and an emphasis on dogmatic correctness and moral compliance linger today in the discipline of ethics, and theologians in CHM have been formed by these factors.[9]

FROM CLINICAL TO ORGANIZATIONAL ETHICS

Alongside the exponential growth of questions involving the clinical practice of medicine, the late twentieth and early twenty-first centuries experienced dramatic developments in regulatory, capitalist,

---

[4] Kevin D. O'Rourke, Thomas Kopfensteiner, and Ron Hamel, "A Brief History: A Summary of the Development of the Ethical and Religious Directives for Catholic Health Services," *Health Progress* 82, no. 6 (2001): 18–21.

[5] Gerald Kelly, *Medico-Moral Problems* (St. Louis: The Catholic Hospital Association, 1958). Other examples include David F. Kelly, *The Emergence of Roman Catholic Medical Ethics in North America: An Historical–Methodological–Biographical Study* (Lewiston: Edwin Mellen Press Ltd., 1978). The author notes how topics of medical-moral discourse shifted from what patients confessed, to rules and commandments, to moral analysis of procedures enacted by physicians.

[6] Eric Marcelo Genilo, *John Cuthbert Ford, SJ: Moral Theologian at the End of the Manualist Era* (Washington, DC: Georgetown University Press, 2007).

[7] Pope Pius XII, *The Human Body: Papal Teachings*, ed. The Monks of Solesmes (Boston: St. Paul Editions, 1960).

[8] John Mahoney, *The Making of Moral Theology: A Study of the Roman Catholic Tradition* (Oxford: Oxford University Press, 1987), 259–301.

[9] In *A History of Catholic Moral Theology in the Twentieth Century: From Confessing Sins to Liberating Consciences* (New York: Continuum, 2010), James F. Keenan most helpfully and clearly delineates the major methodologies and their intellectual champions. Many others, such as Richard McCormick, S.J., Joseph Fuchs, S.J., and Bernard Häring, C.Ss.R., employed other methodologies drawing from values, virtue, scripture, liturgy, and other theological concepts.

and organizational structures impacting the overall landscape of healthcare delivery in the United States. These shifts pushed the theologian into another realm of ethics, namely organization ethics. The passage of Medicare in 1965 markedly altered the structure of American healthcare. Changes continue today at an accelerating pace fueled by the passage of the Affordable Care Act in 2010, and subsequent attempts by congressional factions to repeal or systematically dismantle the legislation. Fears, uncertainty, and capitalists' risk-aversion in health insurance markets and financing structures exacerbate the complex commercial and political environments.

Such structural dynamics prompted CHMs to align with other-than-Catholic partner institutions to expand access to basic health services and gain profitability amidst ever-increasing demand for specialty services. A variety of contractual alignments and corporate commingling caused CHMs to question whether they cooperate with morally objectionable actions of doctors, vendors, or institutions with whom they partnered. Theologians drew from the tradition's long-standing principle of cooperation, although they hesitated since the principle had historically been applied to individuals. No precedent existed for applying it to institutions, such as CHMs. Following a decade of dialogue in the early twenty-first century, American theologians across Catholic healthcare and the academy agreed the principle of cooperation applies to Catholic institutions, although analogously.[10]

The emerging need to evaluate cooperation with partners potentially engaged in wrongdoing spurred a notable growth in the role of the theologian in CHMs. Theologians who initially grappled with clinical procedures and actions involving physicians and patients witnessed their scope of inquiry morph to include the relationship between the entire organizational enterprise and society at large.

Determining cooperation with wrongdoing pertains to the integrity of the organization as a ministry of the Church and to theological scandal. To assist theologians in CHMs, the United States Conference of Catholic Bishops (USCCB) substantially revised and expanded the

---

[10] The Catholic Health Association, *Report on a Theological Dialogue on the Principle of Cooperation*, 2007. See also a revised publication by the Catholic Health Association, *Resources About the Principle of Cooperation for the Catholic Health Ministry* (St. Louis: The Catholic Health Association, 2013). Of the 25 core participants listed in the initial 2007 report, nearly two-thirds were clergy and 44% had ecclesiastical degrees. In 2014 the Congregation for the Doctrine of the Faith responded to questions posed by the United States Conference of Catholic Bishops in "Some Principles for Collaboration with Non-Catholic Entities in the Provision of Health Care Services," *National Catholic Bioethics Quarterly* 14, no. 2 (2014): 337–340.

ERDs in 1994, including the addition of part six, which precisely addressed partnerships.[11] The most recent revision to the ERDs in 2018 pertained solely to part six.[12]

Scrutinizing collaborative ventures against the moral tradition's principle of cooperation with wrongdoing further pigeonholes theology in ethics, at least primarily if not exclusively. After the 1994 overhaul of the ERDs, the three subsequent revisions impacted only clinical or organizational ethics. The revisions reflect the U.S. bishops acting in their teaching authority. They acted with consultation and advisement from theologians. As I conclude the first part of the essay tracing the general contours of this historical pairing of theology with ethics in American Catholic healthcare, I pause briefly to elaborate on the term theologian, before discussing expanding the theologian's influence.

THE THEOLOGIAN IN THE CATHOLIC TRADITION

As St. Anselm concisely stated in the eleventh century, theology is faith seeking understanding. Principally, a theologian is one possessing deep and broad understanding of doctrine and the Christian faith. Besides those exceptional cases when the Church posthumously recognizes an individual as a doctor of the Church, ordained clergy were historically the most learned in theology. Through their office and ministry, they brought understanding to the Christian faith both formally and practically. The term theologian thus applied largely to priests who pursued higher studies or an ecclesiastical degree, thereby preparing them as seminary instructors.

A different example of theologians applying intellectual expertise in service to the Church occurred with the *periti* at the Second Vatican Council. The world's bishops brought their trusted advisors who impacted the Council's enduring works.[13] This example reflects a dynamic between theology and the Church's teaching authority.[14] Today, for example, the International Theological Commission serves a

---

[11] O'Rourke, Kopfensteiner, and Hamel, *A Brief History*, 20.
[12] United States Conference of Catholic Bishops, "Ethical and Religious Directives for Catholic Health Services," Sixth Edition, www.usccb.org/about/doctrine/ethical-and-religious-directives/upload/ethical-religious-directives-catholic-health-service-sixth-edition-2016-06.pdf.
[13] Leo DeClerck, "Le rôle joué par les évêques et periti belges au Concile Vatican II: Deux examples," *Ephemerides Theologicae Louvanienses*, 76, no. 1 (2000): 445–464.
[14] Francis A. Sullivan, *Magisterium: Teaching Authority in the Catholic Church* (Eugene: Wipf and Stock Publishers, 1983).

similar purpose.¹⁵ Its members include lay professors, women religious, as well as priests. *Lumen Gentium's* universal call to holiness catalyzed the movement toward diversification among theologians (no. 39–42). A broadening of experience and intellect deepens the call from *Gaudium et Spes* to discern the signs of the times and to apply the tradition to modern developments and discoveries (no. 45).

As such and at its core, theology reflects upon human life in light of the existence and love of God. Christian theology serves the Church and the lives of the faithful to respond to the unfolding of God's reign of love, justice, and peace amid the world's trials and blessings. The Church insightfully asserts that in times of great spiritual and cultural change an acute need arises for the role of theology (*Donum Veritatis*, no. 1).

Thus, in this present essay the term theologian refers to an individual with extensive, in-depth formal training in Catholic theology and doctrine and experience in the study and life of the Christian faith.¹⁶ This working definition pairs intellectual knowledge of the Christian tradition with individual practice. This means that the theologian actively cultivates a life of faith through personal prayer and active participation in a faith community (*Donum Veritatis*, nos. 8-9).¹⁷ As Hans Urs von Balthasar famously said, he prefers a kneeling theology. The remark connotes active, contemplative, and liturgical dimensions, rather than a mere academic, intellectual exercise.

As the ranks of theologians expanded since the Council to include lay faithful, new areas of inquiry, expertise, methodologies, and insights for CHMs arose. The second part of this essay illuminates how parallel shifts in the role of the theologian and the changing pressures on CHMs warrant a recognition and repositioning of the role of the

---

¹⁵ See Pope Paul VI's letter to Prefect Franjo Cardinal Seper of the Congregation for the Doctrine of the Faith, 11 April 1969; later formalized by Pope John Paul II's Apostolic Letter *Tredecim Anni*.

¹⁶ Formal academic credentials typically attest to levels of successful completion of formal training. Master of Arts degrees represent a foundational understanding of a particular discipline, like theology, religious studies, or spirituality. Yet most masters' degrees lack a depth and expertise, particularly as compared to other advanced degrees. Master of Divinity programs generally require almost triple the hours of other master-level programs. Pontifical or Ecclesiastical degrees, such as the Licentiate in Sacred Theology (STL), enables the individual to function as a theological resource to Catholic seminaries, dioceses, or other Catholic institutions. Terminal degrees, such as a Doctorate in Sacred Theology (STD) or a secular Doctor of Philosophy (PhD) in theology or religious studies, most clearly designate an expert and in-depth knowledge referenced in the working definition for the purposes of this article.

¹⁷ See also James Carroll, who draws insightful parallels between practicing the art of medicine and practicing faith in *Practicing Catholic* (New York: Houghton Mifflin Harcourt, 2009), 10; and Darren M. Henson, "Eucharist as the Heart of the Ministry," in *Incarnate Grace: Perspectives on the Ministry of Catholic Health Care*, ed. Charles Bouchard (St. Louis: The Catholic Health Association, 2017), 169–189.

theologian to far exceed clinical and organizational ethics. I will suggest five areas where the theologian provides an important and unique contribution.

Social Ethics and Healthcare
The breadth and depth of theological social ethics expanded in the decades since the Council. While a part of the ethics wheelhouse, social ethics breaks the methodological mode of problem-analysis-answer, largely a manualist mode of inquiry. Rather, social ethics raises important questions pertaining to human dignity, solidarity, the common good, and justice.[18] The methodological mode for Catholic social ethics often is summarized as see-judge-act (*Mater et Magistra*, no. 236).[19] These and other related themes from the social tradition intimately relate to many facets of a CHM. For example, Pope Saint John XXIII declared a fundamental human right to medical care, rest, and to be cared for in times of ill health, disability, unemployment, widowhood, and old age in his 1963 encyclical *Pacem in Terris* (no. 11). Two decades later Cardinal Joseph Bernardin advanced similar thoughts by promoting a consistent ethics of life.[20] Both the Pontiff and the Chicago Cardinal point toward holistic care. Addressing the root causes of abortion, for example, cannot occur without looking at the structures of sin and injustices in the U.S. health care system and the modern world.

In recent years theologians spurred this connection between social ethics and the tarnished structures of American healthcare.[21] Some in CHMs have incorporated aspects of Catholic social thought and teaching into their work, yet their treatment of it often remains couched in clinical terms and confined to public policy and health reform.[22] An

---

[18] See Meghan Clark, *The Vision of Catholic Social Thought: The Virtue of Solidarity and the Praxis of Human Rights* (Minneapolis: Fortress Press, 2014).
[19] See also, Leonardo Boff and Clodovis Boff, *Introducing Liberation Theology*, trans. Paul Burns (Maryknoll: Orbis Books, 1987).
[20] See Joseph Bernardin, "The Consistent Ethic of Life and Health Care Systems," and "The Consistent Ethic of Life and Health Care Reform," in *Selected Works of Joseph Cardinal Bernardin*, Volume 2, ed. Alphonse P. Spilly (Collegeville: Liturgical Press, 2000).
[21] A good example is Lisa Sowle Cahill's Père Marquette Lecture in Theology published as *Bioethics and the Common Good* (Milwaukee: Marquette University Press, 2004). See also her larger work *Theological Bioethics: Participation, Justice and Change* (Washington, DC: Georgetown University Press, 2005).
[22] For this critique, see Michael R. Panicola, David M. Belde, John Paul Slosar, Mark F. Repenshek, *Health Care Ethics: Theological Foundations, Contemporary Issues, and Controversial Cases* (Winona: Anselm Academic, 2011); Benedict M. Ashley, OP, Jean DeBlois, CSJ, Kevin D. O'Rourke, OP, *Health Care Ethics: A Catholic Theological Analysis*, Fifth Edition (Washington, DC: Georgetown University Press, 2006).

Theologians in Catholic Healthcare Ministries 137

integrated approach would identify a medical issue and the moral dilemma, and amply includes themes from the wider theological and social tradition.[23] However, three factors contribute to the meager application of the social tradition in CHMs. One reason entails training. Some responsible for ethics in CHMs studied at institutions emphasizing bioethics and philosophy. Others may have studied with professors schooled in the manualist or neo-manualist methodology.[24] Training begets areas of comfort and expertise, and theologians may be most comfortable providing moral analyses to discrete and delineated questions. A second reason is that social justice is implied in the charitable acts and structures of the CHM itself. This presumption seemingly absolves CHMs of the need for explicit theological reflection. Third, CHMs, like all contemporary medicine, are unavoidably marked by the effects of modernity. Efficiency, effectiveness, immediate applicability, and even monetization, insuppressibly drive much of the culture. The theologian in a CHM does not enjoy the freedom and protected time to research and write, let alone a paid sabbatical, like those afforded to some colleagues in the academy. There is little perceived value or incentive from the organization for the theologian in a CHM to dream of the impact Catholic social teaching could have on community programs, strategy, advocacy and wider operations.

The lacuna between social ethics and healthcare structures and operations opens avenues for all theologians to grow in partnership. The theologian in CHM encounters unique situations scantly attended to by theological discourse. Burgeoning aspects of the social tradition span a vast range and present opportunities to intersect with CHM. For

---

[23] Maura A. Ryan offers an integrative approach in *Ethics and Economics of Assisted Reproduction: The Cost of Longing* (Washington, DC: Georgetown University Press, 2001). Ryan not only addresses the ethics of assisted reproduction but also examines human dignity, access to care, the common good, human suffering, and freedom. Another example comes from Shawnee M. Daniels-Sykes who envisions addressing racial health disparities with the strength of community and solidarity in "Code Black: A Black Catholic Liberation Bioethics," in *The Journal of the Black Catholic Theological Symposium* 3 (2009): 29-59.

[24] See John M. Travaline and Louise A. Mitchell, ed., *Catholic Witness in Health Care: Practicing Medicine in Truth and Love* (Washington, DC: The Catholic University of America Press, 2017). The final chapter laudably highlights a medical clinic for the poor in Appalachia in Kentucky modeled after a "casa" or a place for the sick and suffering founded by St. Pio of Pietrelcina in Italy. Yet the text lacks engagement with the social tradition. An authentic Catholic witness in health care, as the title asserts, must seriously engage the depths of Catholic social teaching and tradition and not merely medical ethics.

example, the environment (*Laudato Si'*, no. 20, 21, 44), immigration,[25] and racism,[26] all connect to health, as does international financing and foreign labor,[27] foreign mission,[28] global health,[29] artificial intelligence,[30] and more. These issues cause theologians in CHMs to break free of the problem-analysis-solution paradigm and delve more deeply into a pursuit of broader implications of social ethics. No singular response suffices for these complex social and operational topics. This reality, therefore, reveals the need for organizational discernment to guide ministry leaders as health resources move outward beyond hospital rooms and walls to meet God's people on the margins.

Discernment

Discernment is careful attention to the presence or absence of God in making decisions and enacting them. It is particularly necessary at critical junctures in an individual's or organization's life. While the distinction may not be immediately self-evident, it differs from organizational ethics and is broader. The latter originated from and continues to entail moral analysis related to cooperation with wrongdoing. Discernment stretches beyond, questioning where God may be calling the organization to expand the healing ministry of Christ Jesus. For example, a discernment process would guide a CHM considering joining another CHM—a situation presumably absent of moral wrongdoing or scandal. Discernment questions how ought the organization as a ministry act in this particular situation with these particular constraints. A discernment process operationalizes the Church's vision of seeing, hearing, and judging strategic options in light of ministerial identity.[31] It provides a structure for senior leaders, board and sponsor members to tackle complex issues and incorporate pertinent aspects of the Catholic tradition to the matters at hand.

---

[25] Darren M. Henson, "Deportation: A Moral Morass," *Health Progress* 98, no. 4 (2017): 35-40. See also Mark Kuczewski, "Can Medical Repatriation Be Ethical? Establishing Best Practices," *The American Journal of Bioethics* 12, no. 9 (2012): 1-5.
[26] Bryan N. Massingale, *Racial Justice and the Catholic Church* (Maryknoll: Orbis Books, 2010).
[27] Darren M. Henson, "Offshore Outsourcing and Catholic Social Teaching," *Health Progress* 97, no. 5 (2016): 43–47.
[28] Kelly Stuart, "Ethical Concerns with Medical Missions Abroad," *Health Care Ethics USA* 23, no. 4 (2015): 21–24.
[29] Lisa Sowle Cahill, "The Ethics of Coming into the World," presented at the Pontifical Academy for Life, Rome, Italy, June 27, 2018, www.academyforlife.va/content/dam/pav/documenti pdf/2018/Assemblea2018/workshop/03_Cahill - paper June 18 clean copy.pdf.
[30] John Cornwell, "Dangerous Thinking," *The Tablet*, Jan. 6, 2018, 10-12.
[31] For one helpful and comprehensive model see Michael Panicola and Ron Hamel, "Catholic Identity and the Reshaping of Health Care," *Health Progress* 96, no. 5 (2015): 46–56.

Theologians in Catholic Healthcare Ministries 139

Because discernment processes include relevant aspects of the Catholic tradition and the honing of virtues, they necessarily call for the gifts and the role of the theologian. Service to discernment is integral to the vocation of the theologian, whose task is to foster dialogue with the culture. At the same time, "It is important to emphasize that when theology employs the elements and conceptual tools of...other disciplines, discernment is needed" (*Donum Veritatis,* no. 10). Synthesizing and making sense of the truths revealed by reason and by faith is the very work of theology.

The Council articulated a role for the theologian in the Church's dialogue with the modern world. With the Holy Spirit, theologians must "hear, distinguish, and interpret the many voices of our age and judge them in light of the divine word, so revealed truth may be more deeply penetrated, better understood, and set forth to greater advantage" (*Gaudium et Spes,* no. 44). Discernment, conducted with participants open to the Spirit, enables the organization to act with integrity. The process also serves to scrutinize the organizational conscience to then act out of that conscience. Like that of the individual, conscience needs to be formed. Formation, in CHM, emerged when sponsors and leaders saw more clearly the growing need to educate executives and clinical associates alike on foundational matters of Catholic identity and spirituality, and they turned to the Church's tradition of formation.

Formation in CHMs
Amidst the exponentially increasing complexities in healthcare today, CHMs have developed formation programs within mission departments. One of the many aims of formation entails sharpening not merely the knowledge but also the consciousness of leaders and decision-makers in the organization. The development of formation programs opens up an entirely new organizational geography that calls for the gifts and resources of theology. Charles Bouchard, OP, asserts:

> It is clear that there can be no meaningful appropriation of the term 'ministry' to describe Catholic healthcare unless it is nourished with serious theology and spirituality at a number of levels. Senior leaders, board members and sponsors must acquire fluency in theological questions that impact healthcare just as they have fluency in organizational development, finance and strategic planning. They must also see that formation extends across the organization so that all leaders, employees and volunteers grasp the mission and are able to participate actively in it.[32]

---

[32] Charles Bouchard, OP, "The Meaning of Ministry in Health Care," in *Incarnate Grace: Perspectives on the Ministry of Catholic Health Care,* ed. Charles Bouchard (St. Louis: The Catholic Health Association, 2017), 205.

Bouchard's astute observations and deep experience in both theology and Catholic healthcare articulate how formation, as a theological activity, directly and intimately impacts the organization beyond ethics. The latter tends to emerge in times of conflict. Conversely, formation endeavors occur within the ordinary life of the CHM.

Celeste Mueller advances a formation model that comprises both theological foundations and spiritual practices.[33] These twin pillars of theology and spirituality gesture toward von Balthasar's kneeling theology. They represent a post-conciliar motif that formation entails more than knowledge, and Mueller's methodology reflects the Church's view that "theology requires a spiritual effort to grow in virtue and holiness" (*Donum Veritatis*, no. 9). Thus, spiritual practices belong alongside theologically grounded formation.

What exactly ought to constitute formation, theologically and spiritually, remains an open question. Determining a formation program's content and method will involve many voices. Theological expertise ought to be among them. The theologian can contribute in various ways to the creation of formation programs. I highlight two aspects: to foster virtue and to ensure the formation program is consonant with the tradition.

First, formation in CHMs entails individual growth, if not holiness, which in the Christian tradition includes virtue or the practice of benevolent habits.[34] As individuals grow in virtue, so too might the organization act more virtuously. Pope Francis expanded the Council's call to universal holiness in *Gaudete et Exsultate*. The theologian brings knowledge of the depth of the virtue tradition and the role that virtues play in healing and the unfolding of the reign of God. Relatedly, the theologian as one steeped in the tradition can ensure that formation avoids distortions of authentic Christian witness.[35]

Second, formation must bear resonance with the tradition. The Council and official documents since then reimagined religious and priestly formation in light of its call to embrace the modern world,

---

[33] Celeste DeSchryver Mueller, "Formation: Catholic Theology Alive in Catholic Health Care," in *Incarnate Grace: Perspectives on the Ministry of Catholic Health Care*, ed. Charles Bouchard (St. Louis, MO: The Catholic Health Association, 2017), 271–289.

[34] James F. Keenan, S.J., *Virtues for Ordinary Christians* (Lanham: Sheed and Ward, 1996).

[35] Pope Francis, here and in other writings, identifies modern reiterations of Gnosticism and Pelagianism. Both find fertile ground in medicine and the corporate milieu. The former prizes the intellect to the detriment of the body. Though medicine treats the body, the physicians who lead it and the structures that deliver it prize the mind. Contemporary Pelagianism relies on the human will and personal effort. It is especially prevalent in American corporate culture, and ongoing formation ought to provide practices and structures to transcend these tendencies. See *Gaudete et Exsultate*, no. 35–46, and *Evangelii Gaudium*, no. 94, 233.

cognizant of worldly pitfalls. The theologian possesses the expertise and is uniquely adept to interpret and bring such documents' vision to leaders for incorporation into the formative experience. The USCCB's expectation for priestly formation includes four dimensions: human, spiritual, intellectual, and pastoral.[36] As increasing numbers of lay persons entered pastoral ministry, the USCCB issued guidelines for their development, and, quite interestingly, they articulated the same four areas noted for priestly formation.[37]

I am not arguing that CHMs necessarily adopt these aims. Formation must effectively respond to the needs of the ministry. Bouchard, Mueller and others pinpoint unique challenges and requirements of formation in CHMs whose leaders include Catholics and non-Catholics, and whose healing ministry extends far beyond the institutional walls into the fabric of a highly pluralistic society. Just as Bouchard calls for renewed theologies of ministry in light of emerging iterations arising in Catholic healthcare, it is equally important to reimagine formation within the tradition. Formation does not and will not mirror seminary formation, for example, but it must be recognizably Catholic—meaning it clearly relates to and draws from the tradition that speak to formation.

The transition from religious communities to separately constituted public juridic persons that can and do include laypersons precipitated, in part, the request from sponsors themselves for formation. It expressed a desire to entrust essential aspects of the original charism, ethos, and zeal that ultimately arose out of the healing stories of Jesus and have been relived by leading religious women and men throughout the centuries.

Sponsorship

All of the aforementioned areas of a CHM meriting the gifts of the theologian ultimately stand to support and strengthen the work of the governance and sponsorship. Currently, theological expertise may commonly intersect with sponsors through formation to these bodies, and it may additionally entail direct service on particular matters. One could view the early medico-moral analysis by Gerald Kelly as service to the individual congregations sponsoring local hospitals. The religious communities looked to trained theologians to render moral judgments that in turn strengthened the congregation's integrity as ministries enacted in the name of the Catholic Church. In a sense, a renewed

---

[36] See *Program of Priestly Formation,* 5th Edition (Washington, DC: United States Conference of Catholic Bishops, 2006). Also *Optatum Totius,* chapter four, and *Pastores Dabo Vobis* highlight greater attention to spiritual training.
[37] *Co-Workers in the Vineyard of the Lord: A Resource for Guiding the Development of Lay Ecclesial Ministry* (Washington, DC: United States Conference of Catholic Bishops, 2005), 33–53.

focus on theologically supporting sponsors represents a retrieval of an earlier function. At the same time, organizational, clinical, and social ethics, discernment, and formation all serve the sponsors as they forge ahead into new endeavors to heal in complex social and individual realities.

Bouchard observes how sponsorship entails unique canonical and theological roles.[38] It may behoove sponsors to have members who themselves bring a substantial depth of theological training and expertise, as well as search out other voices from the theological community. The theologian's role with sponsorship in turn relates to church relations. Theologians serve the sponsor and senior leaders in their dialogue with bishops and diocesan personnel. Often this may take the form of gradually educating bishops and their representatives on economic, scientific, organizational, and technological matters that press upon a ministry aimed at working within social and cultural confines to tend to the needs of the poor and marginalized. It might also include advising sponsors and leaders on difficult matters. It could even include offering theological reflection on the nature of sponsorship in CHM, a very new theological concept.

Theological Collaboration – CHMs, Academics, and Bishops

Collaboration among theologians entails three spheres—those in CHMs, in diocesan roles, and in the academy. Fruitful collaboration involves a generosity of spirit, which begins with the recognition that each brings unique gifts and insights that can be mutually enriching. Generously listening and understanding the perspective of the other fosters mutual good will. Bouchard witnesses to the type of theological collaboration needed. He noted how practice and language operative in CHMs are ahead of the theology and thus assembled new scholarship for a contemporary Catholic theology of the healing ministry by inviting theologians from the academy and CHM to dialogue via video conference and correspondence. The result was *Incarnate Grace* with a foreward notably penned by a bishop.[39]

Bishops are no strangers to theological quandaries and, as previously noted, their advisors—particularly those designated as liaisons for healthcare—are themselves theologically trained. Dialogue cannot overlook theologians in seminaries, particularly locations preparing students for diocesan ministry. Decades later these seminarians will be priests influencing and advising bishops. The wider the dialogue with an accurate and ongoing articulation of the many challenges of

---

[38] Bouchard, "The Meaning of Ministry in Health Care," 209.
[39] Robert N. Lynch, "Foreward," in *Incarnate Grace: Perspectives on the Ministry of Catholic Health Care*, ed. Charles Bouchard (St. Louis: The Catholic Health Association, 2017), ix.

Theologians in Catholic Healthcare Ministries 143

healing ministries entrenched in the world, and yet not fully of it, will more authentically redound to its benefit and to the work of theology itself.

Also previously noted, a need exists for a more astute sensitivity between CHMs and the academy. On the one hand, the academy can grow in appreciation for the monumental challenges that stymie practical implementation of a broader theological vision for CHMs. One scholar contributor to *Incarnate Grace* remarked how much he learns whenever he interacts with those inside CHM. A spirit of mutual learning and enrichment is helpful in this ongoing dialogue. Academics and chancery personnel alike can underappreciate the difficulties of doing theology in an environment where most are not Catholic, have limited experience with the Catholic world and imagination, and yet have good hearts and a passion for the healing ministry, and seek to do what is best in difficult circumstances and in an environment and industry that scarcely harnesses modernity's forces.

On the other hand, if theologians in CHMs are the ones entrenched in the missionary-like environment of modernity-laden medicine practiced within the unforgiving confines of the American political and regulatory environment, then we need to articulate our reality more accurately and loudly so that those in different settings can better assist us. For example, in recent years both CHMs and universities have called for greater access to fellowships. Training and preparing young theologians for work in CHM must remain a priority for both. Advisors to these students must be acutely cognizant that students' own formation cannot be exclusively intellectual.

Theology is always a response to God's action. It happens after the Spirit of God has swept by us. As CHMs and the multiple gears that operate the structure of health care in the U.S. evolve, theologians have much work and contemplation. With prayer, an active life of faith, and scholarship rooted deeply in the riches of the Church and a post-conciliar theology, theologians can make meaningful and lasting contributions to CHMs especially for its sponsors, the people and communities served, and for the whole of the Church itself.

CONCLUSION

Moving more fully into a wider landscape where theologians in CHM have the freedom to contribute across disciplines requires embracing a full vision of the Council—one of continual *ressourcement* along with the continual *aggiornamento* present in medicine. No longer can mission leaders, senior leaders, and sponsors typecast theologians as ethicists or even moral theologians. The serious and contemporary challenges of CHMs call out for the very best across a broader theological spectrum ranging from social ethics and pastoral theology to ecclesiology, missiology, sacramental-liturgical theology, spirituality, anthropology, canon law, biblical studies, and more. An authentic *ressourcement* to advance CHMs necessitates more than mere exposure to theology. It requires advanced degrees and commitments from theologians for life-long learning. Lastly, it will require the virtue of humility. No one person and no one discipline holds the single solution to these vexing issues of fostering a Catholic healing ministry in a contemporary, pluralistic society. It calls for community and a kneeling theology, where the theologian is nourished by the living presence of God encountered in the people, word, and sacrament at the eucharistic celebration, to then embrace *aggiornamento*—sent out again to be God's very presence in word, thought, and deed. Ⓜ

CONTRIBUTORS

Rachelle Barina, PhD, is Vice President of Mission Integration at SSM Health. She also has an academic appointment in the Albert Gnaegi Center for Health Care Ethics at St. Louis University.

Becket Gremmels, PhD, is the System Director of Ethics for CHRISTUS Health, a Catholic health system based in Irving, Texas. Before that, he was the Executive Director of Ethics for Saint Thomas Health in Nashville, Tennessee, and St. Vincent's Health Services in Birmingham, Alabama. He completed a fellowship in clinical ethics at Saint Thomas West Hospital in Nashville. He received his PhD in Health Care Ethics from the Albert Gnaegi Center for Health Care Ethics at Saint Louis University. He and his wife have been married for 11 years and have three children.

Darren M. Henson, PhD, STL, is Vice President of Mission and Discernment at Presence Health in Chicago, now a part of Ascension. He received his PhD in religious studies at Marquette University with specialization in theological ethics and Catholic healthcare. He previously earned a pontifical Licentiate in Sacred Theology and a Master of Divinity from the University of St. Mary of the Lake.

Nathaniel Hibner is Director of Ethics for The Catholic Health Association of the United States. He is also an Instructor in Organizational Ethics for the Aquinas Institute of Theology.

Conor Kelly is an assistant professor in the department of theology at Marquette University. His teaching and research focuses on ways theology can provide resources for ethical discernment in ordinary life. His academic writings have appeared in a variety of publications, including *Theological Studies*, the *Journal of the Society of Christian Ethics*, and the *Journal of Catholic Social Thought*. He recently authored a chapter on Christology and Catholic health care, published in *Incarnate Grace: Perspectives on the Ministry of Catholic Health Care* (CHA USA, 2017).

Ramon Luzarraga is Assistant Professor of Theology and Department Chair of theology and philosophy at Benedictine University Mesa in Arizona. He also serves on the board of directors of the Society of Christian Ethics.

M. Therese Lysaught, PhD, is Professor of Catholic moral theology and health care ethics at the Institute of Pastoral Studies at Loyola University Chicago, with a secondary appointment in the Neiswanger Institute for Bioethics at Loyola's Stritch School of Medicine. In addition to consulting with health care systems on issues surrounding mission, theology, and ethics, her major research foci have included the anointing of the sick, genetics, gene therapy, human embryonic stem cell research and issues at the end-of-life. Her books include: *Catholic Bioethics and Social Justice: The Praxis of U.S. Health Care in a Globalized World* (Liturgical Press, 2018, co-editor Michael P. McCarthy); *Caritas in Communion: Theological Foundations of Catholic Health Care* (St. Louis: Catholic Health Association); *On Moral Medicine: Theological Perspectives on Medical Ethics*, 3rd edition (Eerdmans, 2012, co-edited with Joseph Kotva); and *Gathered for the Journey: Moral Theology in Catholic Perspective* (Eerdmans, 2007, co-editor David M. McCarthy).

Michael McCarthy, PhD, is an Assistant Professor at the Neiswanger Institute for Bioethics at Loyola University Chicago Stritch School of Medicine where he co-directs the Physician's Vocation Program, which seeks to ground the formation of medical students in the Spiritual Exercises of St. Ignatius Loyola. He co-edited, with Therese Lysaught, *Catholic Bioethics and Social Justice: The Praxis of U.S. Health Care in a Globalized World* (Liturgical Press, 2018). He has published and presented on the role of justice in bioethics, the importance of spirituality in patient care and medical education, clinical ethics, and ethics consultation.

Cory D. Mitchell is a graduate of the Health Care Mission Leadership program at the Loyola University Chicago Institute of Pastoral Studies and current doctoral candidate at the Loyola University Chicago Neiswanger Institute for Bioethics and Health Policy. Having served in the U.S. Navy, as a research intern at Johns Hopkins University's Bloomberg School of Public Health, and a Program Specialist Intern at the National Institutes of Health Institute on Aging, he has significant experience working with vulnerable populations, including veterans and the homeless. As an African American, his research interests are Catholic health care, health disparities, and theological ethics.

Michael Panicola, PhD, is a bioethicist and a principal at Third View Advisors in St. Louis, Missouri, which he founded after having worked previously as a senior executive in Catholic healthcare for two decades.

Tobias Winright is the Hubert Mäder Endowed Associate Professor of Health Care Ethics in the Gnaegi Center for Health Care Ethics at Saint Louis University, where he is also Associate Professor of Theological Ethics in the Department of Theological Studies. His teaching and research focus on fundamental moral theology and applied ethical issues concerning bioethics, war and peace, criminal justice, and the environment. He has coauthored, edited, or coedited five books: *After the Smoke Clears: The Just War Tradition and Post War Justice* (Orbis, 2010), *Green Discipleship: Catholic Theological Ethics and the Environment* (Anselm Academic, 2011), *Violence, Transformation and the Sacred: "They Shall be Called Children of God"* (Orbis, 2012), *Environmental Justice and Climate Change: Assessing Pope Benedict XVI's Ecological Vision for the Catholic Church in the United States* (Lexington, 2013), and *Can War Be Just in the 21st Century: Ethicists Engage the Tradition* (Orbis, 2015). He was coeditor of the *Journal of the Society of Christian Ethics* from 2013 to 2017. He received his PhD from the University of Notre Dame and his MDiv from Duke Divinity School.

Paul J. Wojda is associate professor of theology at the University of St. Thomas. He received his PhD in Christian Ethics/Moral Theology from the University of Notre Dame in 1993. Since 2011 he has helped facilitate discussions about Catholic identity, using the "Catholic Identity Matrix," developed by Ascension Health and the University of St. Thomas, at more than thirty Catholic hospitals/health care systems across the United States, Mexico, and South America.

STUDENT INTERNS

Patrick T. Fitzgerald, C'19 Mount St. Mary's University, is from Calverton, NY, and is earning a double major in Theology and Philosophy.

Sydney D. Johnson, C'19 Mount St. Mary's University, majoring in Philosophy with minors in History and Spanish, is from Lincoln, NE.

COVER ART

"The Maid of Lorraine," by **Sarah Hunter**, a graduate of Saint Vincent College, Latrobe, PA. www.thecensoredartist.com.

Articles available to view
or download at:

www.msmary.edu/jmt

The

Journal of Moral Theology

is proudly sponsored by

The College of Liberal Arts
at
Mount St. Mary's University

www.ingramcontent.com/pod-product-compliance
Lightning Source LLC
Chambersburg PA
CBHW051943160426
43198CB00013B/2276